Benzie County Michigan
Rivers, Lakes, and Creeks

Explore *fishing* and *paddling* the wonderful inland
water of this favorite northwestern Michigan area.

By Jim Stamm

• Second Edition •

A hearty "thank you very much!" to all who contributed to make this book possible and helped to improve its presentation. Special recognition and appreciation goes to Donald P. Mead for his significant contribution and invaluable assistance throughout this project. A grateful "thank you!" to Bryce Robison for the project's original concept and his help and encouragement along the way.

A Guide to Benzie County Michigan Rivers, Lakes, and Creeks

Explore *fishing* and *paddling* the wonderful inland water of this favorite northwestern Michigan area.

Second Edition (2.4, n105)

This book and all photos © copyright 2014 by Jim Stamm. All rights reserved.

ISBN-13: 978-1480101821

ISBN-10: 1480101826

Photos used:
- front cover — "Pterodactyl's Retreat" (color) at Mary's Lake
- title page — "Pterodactyl's Retreat" (B & W) at Mary's Lake
- page 4 — "Herring Creek at Upper Herring Lake, #2"
- page 128 — "Afterglow" (black & white) on Crystal Lake
- back cover — "Afterglow" (color) on Crystal Lake

About the author — *Jim Stamm has a B.S. in physics, a minor in mathematics, and 15 years experience with Motorola as a quartz crystal design and software engineer. His love for the outdoors brought him to northwestern Michigan. In 1996 his fondness for teaching and working with computers led him to start ATI Consulting (www.ATIC.biz), a computer consulting and Web site design company.*

At the Web page for this book — **atic.biz/bc_water_guide.html** — are details about where this book can be found locally, on Amazon, and via book distributors, as well as links to many more rivers and creeks in the northwestern Michigan area.

Table of Contents

ABOUT THIS GUIDE 5
BENZIE COUNTY INLAND WATER MAP — WEST 6
BENZIE COUNTY INLAND WATER MAP — EAST 7
FISHING IN BENZIE COUNTY 9
FISH TYPICALLY CAUGHT AT A GLANCE 12
PADDLING IN BENZIE COUNTY 13
RIVERS 14
KNOW YOUR RIVER 14
KNOW YOUR BRIDGES 15
RIVERS AT A GLANCE 17
   1. Betsie River 18
   2. Upper Platte River 41
   3. Lower Platte River 45
CREEKS 53
CREEKS AT A GLANCE 53
   1. Deadstream 53
   2. Grass Lake Creek 55
   3. Herring Creek 57
   4. Otter Creek 60
   5. Pickerel Creek 62
INLAND LAKES 65
INLAND LAKES AT A GLANCE 66
   1. Bass Lake 67
   2. Betsie Lake (a.k.a. Betsie Bay) 68
   3. Bronson Lake 71
   4. Brooks Lake 73
   5. Cook Lake 75
   6. Crystal Lake 76
   7. Davis Lake 82
   8. Deer Lake 83
   9. Fuller Lake 85
  10. Garey Lake 86
  11. Grass Lake 88
  12. Herendeene Lake 89

TABLE OF CONTENTS (continued)

13. LAKE ANN 91
14. LIME LAKE 93
15. LITTLE PLATTE LAKE 96
16. LONG LAKE 97

17. LOON LAKE 98
18. LOWER HERRING LAKE 100
19. MARY'S LAKE 103
20. MUD LAKE (OFF OF LAKE ANN) 104

21. MUD LAKE (NEAR THE LOWER PLATTE RIVER) 106
22. MUD LAKE (OFF OF SANFORD LAKE) 109
23. OTTER LAKE 110
24. PEARL LAKE 112

25. PLATTE LAKE 114
26. ROUND LAKE 117
27. SANFORD LAKE 119
28. STEVENS LAKE 120

29. TURTLE LAKE 122
30, 31. TWIN / UPPER TWIN LAKES 123
32. UPPER HERRING LAKE 125

A PLACE FOR YOUR NOTES 128

- Page 4 -

ABOUT THIS GUIDE

Michigan has more than 11,000 lakes and ponds and over 36,000 miles of rivers and streams (12,000 miles of which are cold-water trout streams). Despite being the smallest county in the state, Benzie County — in northwestern lower Michigan — is "big" on water. It has 58 inland lakes, 100 miles of rivers, and many creeks and streams. It also has 25 miles of Lake Michigan shoreline. This guide covers 32 of the county's 58 inland lakes, two of its four rivers, and five of its many creeks.

This book is a quick and handy reference for *fishing by boat* and *paddling* many of the inland lakes and waterways of Benzie County. It is NOT a "how to fish" or a "how to paddle" guide. It IS a guide for where the water is, how to get there, and what to expect once there. It's intended for those with a small-water craft — such as a bass boat, drift boat, small fishing boat, row boat, canoe, or kayak.

This guide does not cover all the lakes, rivers, and creeks in the county. It's limited to those that are publicly and easily accessible and navigable, and those on which a small boat is allowed and is practical. In all cases access to the water is by car/truck but may involve carrying your boat a short distance. A few lakes can only be accessed via other waterways.

The maps on the following two pages show the location of the lakes, rivers, and creeks covered in this guide and the major roads around them. Detailed road directions to boat launches and access points are provided in the details for each body of water. A good Benzie County road map is recommended if you're not familiar with the area or the roads involved. For each access site GPS coordinates are provided as well as Google Maps links (which are usable on any device with Internet access).

Benzie County Inland Water Map — West

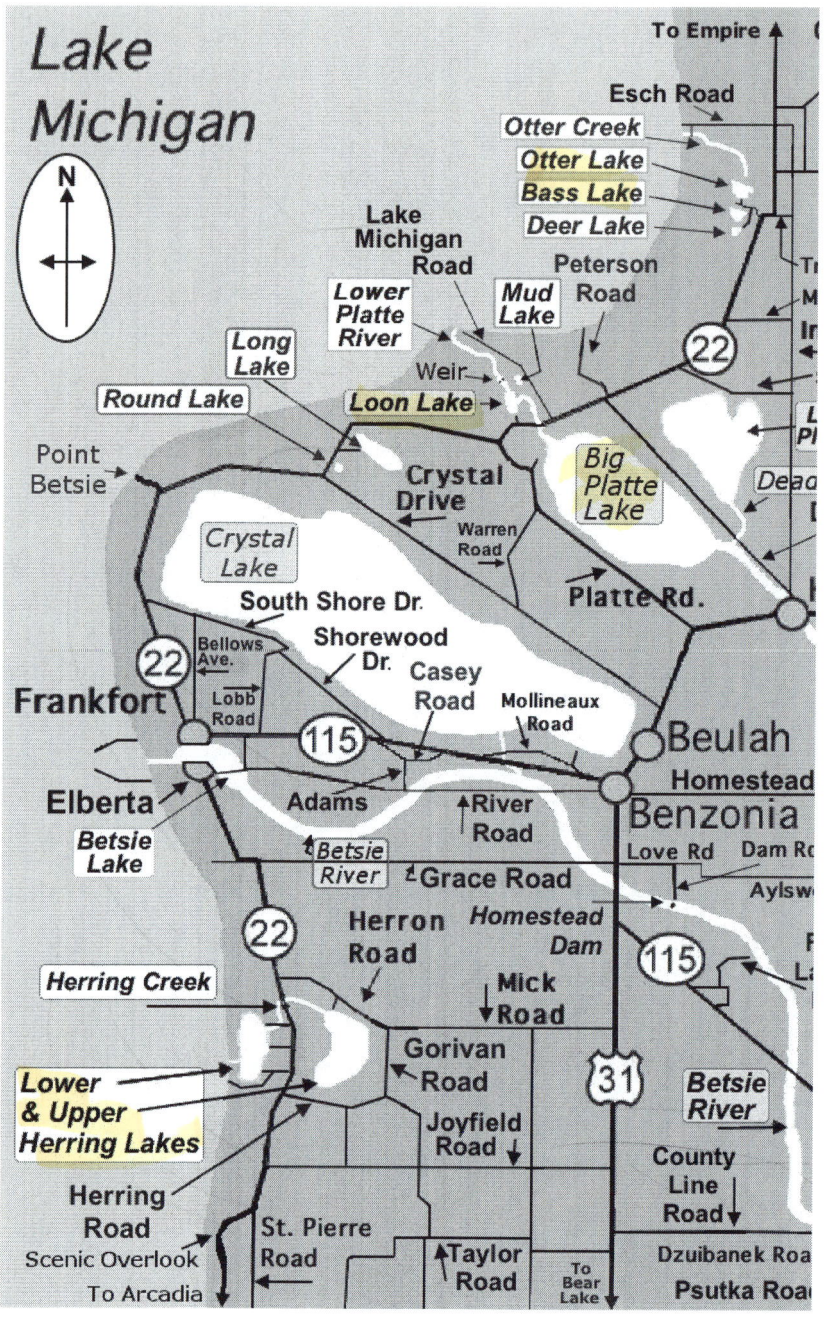

Benzie County Inland Water Map — East

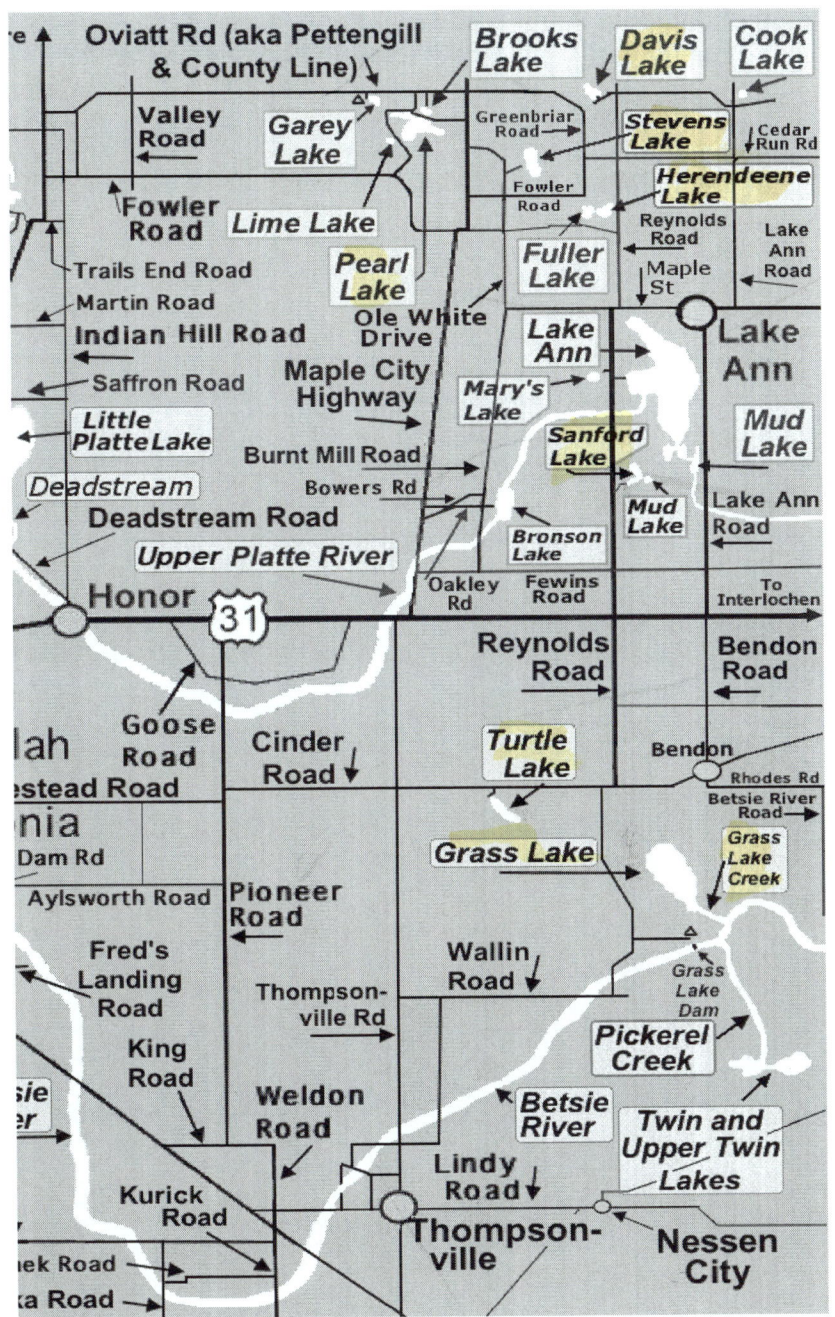

About the details in this guide:

- Links to all Web addresses in this book are available on one convenient Web page: **atic.biz/bciw_links.html**
- Addresses for Web pages and maps can be viewed in any Web browser on any device with Internet access.
- All external Web addresses were correct at the time of writing but note that some are subject to change.
- The **DNR maps** of lakes were made in the 1950s and 1960s and some of their data is even older, so it may be out-of-date. Although the size and depths of the lakes have not changed very much, several of the roads have — they've changed names, moved, or been added since those maps were created.
- **Paddle times** are estimates based on a combination of steady paddling and floating. The times will vary based on the boat being used, how much and how fast you paddle, and the height and speed of the river. Pure floaters can add up to 30% to the paddle times given.
- For the **Fish typically caught** category for each body of water, this guide provides the game fish most often sought and usually caught.
- Some specifics about **where fish are typically found** are offered for many lakes, mostly the larger ones. Information about where specific fish species are found in general is offered in the FISH TIPS sprinkled throughout the INLAND LAKES section.
- **Carry-in access** means only boats you can carry (such as car-top boats, canoes, and kayaks) may be launched at that location.
- Access at a particular **corner** at a river access point means the corner of the intersection of the road and the river.
- **Directions** usually start from the nearest Benzie County town.
- Road distances are estimates.

> Although many areas run by the Michigan DNR require a Michigan Recreational Passport, **none** of the areas or sites in the guide have such a requirement. See this page for details: **michigan.gov/recreationpassport**

> **NOTE:** The use of any area in the Sleeping Bear Dunes National Lakeshore requires a national park pass. In this guide the following areas are in the National Lakeshore: Bass Lake, Deer Lake, Loon Lake, Mud Lake (near the Lower Platte River), Otter Lake, Round Lake, Otter Creek, and most of the Lower Platte River. More details about national park passes are available here:
> nps.gov/slbe/planyourvisit/feesandreservations.htm

FISHING in BENZIE COUNTY

At only 316 square miles, Benzie County is the smallest county in Michigan, yet it's huge with fishing possibilities. The county is home to some of the Midwest's most renowned trout, salmon, and steelhead streams. Often called a fisherman's paradise, there is no end to the fishing opportunities in the county, ranging from "big-water" fishing on Lake Michigan to exploring the county's many creeks and streams. Here you can:

- Explore sport-fishing for salmon, trout, and steelhead on Lake Michigan via a charter service or your own big-water vessel from the Frankfort-Elberta Harbor.
- Take advantage of local fishing guide services on the many inland lakes and waterways.
- Fish the mouth of the Platte and Betsie Rivers or Lake Michigan from the piers — especially during the "runs" in the spring and fall.
- Pull on waders and explore fishing along (or in) the four rivers and many creeks.
- Test your ice fishing skills on the county's 58 inland lakes including Betsie Bay.
- Arm yourself with this book and a small-water craft, kayak, or canoe and explore many of the county's rivers, creeks, and inland lakes.

The DNR says, "Michigan has around 146 kinds of fish, ranging from tiny minnows to giant lake sturgeon." For details on these fish and the best ways to catch them, see:

Michigan Fish and How to Catch Them
michigan.gov/dnr/0,4570,7-153-10364_52261-213908--,00.html

Find out about fish stocked in Michigan waters since 1979 at this helpful page:

Fish Stocking Database — michigandnr.com/fishstock

Many of the game fish found in Michigan abound in Benzie County, including:

- A late summer/early fall run of chinook (king) and coho salmon at Lake Michigan and in the two main rivers.
- A late fall through spring spawning run of steelhead from Lake Michigan into the rivers.
- An April through June run of white sucker in Betsie Bay, the rivers, and some of the inland lakes.
- Bass, brown trout, northern pike, perch, rainbow trout, and sunfish in the rivers.
- Bluegill, brown trout, channel catfish, (black) crappie, lake trout, lake whitefish, largemouth bass, northern pike, (yellow) perch, pumpkin-seed, rainbow trout, rock bass, smallmouth bass, smelt, and walleye in the inland lakes.

Besides game fish there also are several types of "rough fish" found generally throughout the county, such as bullhead, carp, dogfish, gar, and redhorse.

This book does not cover all known species in a body of water, but only those game fish most often sought and typically caught.

You've heard the explanation for when you're not even getting a nibble — "that's why it's called *fishing* not *catching*." Much of the fun of fishing is the uncertainty and unexpected surprises. But in Benzie County the fish are almost always biting somewhere — so here it's been said, "If you're not catching — you're not trying!"

For more information and detail about the two main rivers and 14 of the larger lakes in Benzie County, including depth contours and lake structures, see the *"Sportsman's Connection — Northwest Michigan Fish Map Guide"* available at local retailers and online.

Michigan requires a fishing license for those 17 years of age or older who plan on fishing the state's world-class waters. Fishing licenses are available at many local retailers. Those shops will also have information about fishing seasons, size and quantity limits, regulations, and restrictions. They can help with bait, tackle, equipment, the latest on what's biting, on what, and where.

Details about Michigan fishing licenses, seasons, and regulations are provided at this DNR Web page:

Michigan Fishing Licenses, Seasons, and Regulations
michigan.gov/dnr/0,4570,7-153-10364_63235---,00.html

Those fishing with boats in Michigan will appreciate this Web site:

Michigan DNR's Boating Information System
mcgi.state.mi.us/mrbis

It provides details about Michigan boating access sites, harbors, and marinas. The "Go to the Map Page" link provides details and a road map for each of Michigan's boat launch locations. Or, click on the "Fishing" tab for lots of information about fish and fishing in Michigan.

All anglers and boaters need to be aware of this Michigan DNR Web page:

Preventing the spread of fish diseases and nuisance species
michigan.gov/dnr/0,1607,7-153-10364-160949--,00.html

It points out the very important role anglers and boaters play in the prevention process. The Web page provides the several steps required and more information on the subject. Properly "cleaning boats, trailers, and other equipment thoroughly between fishing trips to keep from transporting undesirable fish pathogens and organisms from one water body to another" is perhaps the most important step. Be aware that Michigan law prohibits placing a boat, trailer, or other boating equipment into Michigan waters with any plant material attached.

FISH TYPICALLY CAUGHT at a GLANCE

Benzie County River or Lake	Bluegill	Brown Trout	Channel Catfish	Crappie	Largemouth Bass	Lake Trout	Lake Whitefish	Northern Pike	Perch	Rainbow/Steelhead	Rock Bass	Salmon	Smallmouth Bass	Smelt	Sunfish	Walleye	White Sucker
Betsie River	X	X			X			X	X	X	X	X					X
Upper Platte River		X								X		X					X
Lower Platte River		X			X			X		X		X	X				X
Bass Lake	X				X			X	X		X		X				
Betsie Lake	X	X	X		X			X	X	X	X	X				X	X
Bronson Lake	X			X	X			X	X		X						
Brooks Lake	X			X	X				X								
Cook Lake	X			X	X				X		X						
Crystal Lake	X	X				X	X	X	X	X	X	X	X				X
Davis Lake	X				X			X	X		X						
Deer Lake	X				X			X	X		X		X				
Fuller Lake	X			X	X				X		X						
Garey Lake	X			X	X			X	X		X						
Grass Lake	X				X			X	X								
Herendeene Lk	X			X	X				X		X						
Lake Ann	X	X		X	X			X	X	X	X		X		P		
Lime Lake	X				X			X	X		X					X	
Little Platte Lake	X			X	X			X	X		X				P		
Long Lake	X				X			X	X		X						
Loon Lake	X			X	X			X	X	X	X	X	X		R		
Lower Herring Lk	X				X			X	X	X	X	X				X	X
Mary's Lake	X				X												
Mud Lake (off of Lake Ann)	X			X	X				X								
Mud Lake (near Lower Platte Rvr)					X												
Mud Lake (off of Sanford Lake)	X				X			X	X		X				G		
Otter Lake	X				X			X	X		X		X				
Pearl Lake	X			X	X			X	X		X						
Platte Lake	X	X	X	X	X			X	X	X	X	X	X		P	X	
Round Lake	X				X				X		X				GP		
Sanford Lake	X				X			X	X		X				G		
Stevens Lake	X			X	X				X		X						
Turtle Lake	X			X	X			X	X		X					X	
Twin / Upper Lks	X				X			X	X		X						
Upper Herring Lk	X			X	X			X	X		X					X	

Sunfish — **G**: green sunfish, **P**: pumpkinseed, **R**: redear sunfish

PADDLING in BENZIE COUNTY

There are many paddling opportunities in the county.

- Sea kayakers can take on "the big lake" — Lake Michigan — from Arcadia to Empire. Along the way you'll find the Sleeping Bear Dunes National Lakeshore, beautiful sandy bluffs and beaches, Frankfort and Point Betsie Lighthouses, harbors at Arcadia and Frankfort, and the mouths of the Lower Herring Lake outlet, the Platte River, and Otter Creek.

- Recreational river paddlers will enjoy the two main rivers, both Class I (the only type of water in the county):
    - The two sections of the one-day-long Platte River — the faster, narrower, and trickier Upper Platte (from east of Honor to Platte Lake), and the quieter and easy Lower Platte (from Platte Lake to Lake Michigan).
    - The moderately easy, three-day-long Betsie River that runs from near Interlochen to Lake Michigan.

- Explorers can check out the several quiet and easy creeks, all in wonderful wild areas.

- Inland lake paddlers can investigate many of the county's inland lakes, ranging from the nearly 10,000 acre Crystal Lake to calm, quiet, and wooded lakes just a few acres in size.

This guide covers the last three — the rivers, creeks, and inland lakes of the county.

There are several local businesses and boat liveries that can help with all your boating and equipment needs, as well as help shuttle cars, people, and equipment.

For river and creek paddlers, see this Web page atic.biz/river_log.html for more details and updates to Benzie County rivers and creeks, as well as many rivers and creeks in adjacent counties, several within an hour.

RIVERS

There are four rivers in Benzie County: Betsie, Little Betsie, North Branch Platte River, and the (main) Platte River. The Little Betsie River and North Branch Platte River are more like long creeks and are too narrow and tree-filled to paddle; they are not covered in this guide. On the other hand, the Betsie River is quite long, has many nice sections to explore, and takes many pages in this guide. The (main) Platte River is also covered — it's divided into the Upper and Lower sections which are quite different from each other and separated by the large Platte Lake.

Know Your River

The Betsie and Platte Rivers covered in this guide are both relatively mild — neither are even Class I. But there are inherent dangers in any river. And **rivers change** — from year to year, season to season, and even within days or hours (after severe weather, for example).

So it's imperative that you know beforehand the difficulty and current condition of the section of the river you are about to paddle. Be sure you and everyone in your group is able to handle the conditions and the known challenges of the river, as well as prepared for the unexpected.

The biggest concerns are tree-fall and log jams in and/or across the river, and in front of culverts. These are usually the worst in the spring after a hard winter has brought down many trees, and after the water has been high and moved and piled loose logs and tree-fall, such as in the spring and during severe or long rainy periods.

Local liveries typically clear some of the more popular river sections, but do not rely on that. In addition, some sections are cleared only occasionally — perhaps by fishing guide services or helpful individuals and organizations. (A good example seems to be the Upper Betsie above King Road.) And "clear" usually means only that there's a path wide enough for a canoe or kayak. (As you can see, having a bow saw along and doing a little "trimming" can go a long way.)

Therefore, before you go, it's recommended that you scout the river section you're about to do and make sure you know...

- the current height and speed of the river.
- if there are any log jams or piles of tree-fall that require significant maneuvering around or portaging.
- of there are any other (known or recently developed) obstructions or impediments.
- if there are any bridges, and if so. are they platform or culvert-type bridges? The following "Know Your Bridges" section will help.
- if there are any low-clearance platform bridges (such as Nostwick Road on the Betsie River), and can you and all in your party get under them.
- if there are any culverts, and are they completely clear, both inside and several feet before the entrance and after the exit.
- if a portage is even possible where required due to an obstruction.
- to bring along at least one bow saw. We've avoided several "messy" portages with about 10 minutes of work clearing a path through tree-fall or log jams. Know that you are also helping fellow paddlers (and yourself) for years to come.

Once on the water, always look through culverts and under bridges before entering to make sure it's clear all the way through and significantly beyond the end. Can all in your party make it through easily? Be prepared to portage, just in case.

Know Your Bridges

As mentioned above, you should scout the section of river you are about to do. Part of that is knowing the bridges involved and the potential hazards that can be present.

Listed in the tables below are the bridges for both rivers, their type, and additional helpful comments. Culvert-type bridges especially need to be investigated before getting on the river. The Nostwick Road bridge on the upper Betsie has very low clearance at high and average river levels.

Betsie River Bridges	Type	No. of culverts	Culvert size	Comments
• Betsie River Rd	C	1	XL	Unlikely to be clogged.
• Reynold Road	P	n/a	n/a	One support, stay to the left.
• Old Railroad Br	T	n/a	n/a	Many left-over trestles.
• Nostwick Road	P	n/a	n/a	**Very low** clearance at high & average river levels. One support, stay to the right.
• Wallin Road	C	2	Lg	Very tricky if right tube clogged, as left approach channel not navigable.
• Private Bridge	P	n/a	n/a	
• Carmean Road	P	n/a	n/a	
• T'ville Road	C	2	Lg	A.K.A. County Road 669
• King Road	P	n/a	n/a	One support
• Wolf Road	P	n/a	n/a	
• Lindy Road	C	2	Lg	
• M-115 (#1)	P	n/a	n/a	
• Kurick Road	C	4	Med	Only left tube open (2014)
• Psutka Road	P	n/a	n/a	One support
• County Line Rd	C	2	Lg	
• Old King Road	F	n/a	n/a	
• M-115 (#2)	P	n/a	n/a	
• US-31	P	n/a	n/a	
• Grace Road	C	3	Lg	Far left tube blocked
• River Rd (East)	C	2	Lg	Use left tube
• River Rd (West)	P	n/a	n/a	One support
• Elb. Railroad Br	T	n/a	n/a	A few trestles
• M-22 (Lake St)	P	n/a	n/a	Many posts for fishing dock. Low clearance in high water.

Bridge type: C: Culvert, P: Platform, T: Trestle, F: Footbridge

Upper Platte River Bridges	Type	No. of culverts	Culvert size	Comments
• Haze Road	P	n/a	n/a	
• Jean Lane	P	n/a	n/a	
• Pioneer Road	C	2	Lg	
• South Street	C	2	Lg	Use the right tube
• Henry Street	P	n/a	n/a	One timber trestle support
• US-31 Bridge	P	n/a	n/a	
• Indian Hill Road	C	2	Lg	
Bridge type: C: Culvert, P: Platform				

Lower Platte River Bridge — This river has only one bridge at M-22. It's a platform bridge and is kept clear. Also, most paddle trips start below this bridge.

> **PADDLE TIP**: Kayakers — before paddling, be sure to adjust your **foot braces** so your feet and legs are in a comfortable position and your knees or thighs are snugly "locked" in place against the side, cockpit edge. or **thigh/knee braces** of the boat. This offers great control of the boat in challenging circumstances, such as a tipping situation allowing you to balance the boat with a quick snap of your hips.

Rivers at a Glance

Benzie County River	Navigable Length (mi)	Paddle Time, one-way (hrs)	Average Depth (feet)	Width (feet)	Difficulty	Gradient (feet per mile)	Number of Access Points
1. Betsie River	54	18-27	2	20-70	Mod. Easy	5	20
2. Upper Platte	9.0	3.0	1.5	15-70	Inter.	13	2
3. Lower Platte	4.6	2.5	2	50-100	Easy	3	6
• Mod. Easy — Moderately Easy • Inter. — Intermediate							

1. Betsie River

General location: The river travels generally east to west across the entire southern half of the county.

General description: Small, beautiful, long, and winding, this river is three days long and relatively easy to paddle its entire length. A protected trout stream, this river is also designated by the state as a Natural, Scenic, and Wildlife River.

The Betsie River starts at Duck Lake (east of Interlochen in Grand Traverse County), flows through Green Lake, spends most its time in Benzie County, dips briefly through northern Manistee County, and flows all the way to Lake Michigan (via Betsie Lake).

Although much of the three mile section from Duck Lake to Green Lake is not navigable, the majority of the river is. The travelable portion starts at Green Lake in Grand Traverse County. The river is mostly in the woods with just a sprinkling of cottages and a few small campgrounds and resorts along the way. There's open wetland near the beginning of the river around Grass Lake and at the end where it flows through the Betsie River State Game Refuge. It empties into Betsie Lake (a.k.a. Betsie Bay and Frankfort Harbor). There are two dams along the way with easy portages and several road bridges to go under, most with "tube" type culverts.

> A **side excursion** on the Betsie River but outside the scope of this book — put in at Green Lake's Diamond Park Road access and paddle north along the shore 0.2 miles to the inlet of the Betsie River, then explore upriver. One can go almost a mile and along the way encounter the creek which comes in from Bridge Lake and Betsie Creek (which comes in via Tuller's Lake from Cedar Hedge Lake). There are a few fallen trees to maneuver around or "scootch" over. There are also many sizes and kinds of minnows. It's a beautiful wild area.

Major tributaries: (Starting at Green Lake) Hall Creek, Grass Lake Creek (outlet for Grass Lake), Pickerel Creek (outlet for Twin and Upper Twin Lakes), Little Betsie River,

Dair Creek, Rice Creek, and the Crystal Lake Outlet. Note that Grass Lake Creek and Pickerel Creek are paddle-able and covered in the CREEKS section of this guide. The Crystal Lake outlet is too shallow for boats except for a few hundred feet at the end.

Map: The following map of the Betsie River starts at the Grass Lake Dam (skipping the sections above Grass Lake) and shows some of the river's tributaries:

   atic.biz/water_maps/betsie_river.pdf

Length: 60 miles. But the navigable portion, from Green Lake to Betsie Lake, is 54 miles.

Total paddle time: 18 to 27 hours

Depth: Perhaps an average of 2 feet, with some scattered deep and quiet holes, long runs, and nice riffles. Expect higher water in the spring and after heavy rains. Some scattered patches of the river can get down to less than 4 inches deep during hotter/drier summer months. At the outside of some of the turns there are nice "holes" several feet deep. Expect good fishing here and maybe swimming, too — both on purpose and by accident if you're not paying attention.

Width: Generally 20 to 100 feet wide. There are a few locations with islands and narrow channels on each side. Very near the end the river widens out and divides into several channels.

Type of water and difficulty: Class I, moderately easy most of the way. Many sections are OK for novice paddlers, but a few areas require a more advanced touch to maneuver around trees or other obstacles in the water. The average gradient (drop of the river) is 5 feet per mile. On some upper portions the drop is little more than average, and for the initial and final few miles the gradient is much less.

Key obstructions: Being mostly in the woods, there can be "sweepers" — see the following Paddle Tip.

> **PADDLE TIP**: **Sweepers** — low-hanging branches that can "sweep" you from your boat — can be anywhere along wooded rivers. They are common (and more dangerous) at the outside of turns, as the current is usually stronger there and it wants to pull you to the outside and into any obstructions or sweepers. So be sure to continually look ahead so you can maneuver to avoid these **well in advance.**

There can be plenty of tree-fall in the river and in a few cases across the river requiring climbing over or portaging around. There are a few boulders, and watch for occasional submerged limbs and "deadheads" (large, old-growth logs that never made it to the mill) stuck in the bottom but can lurk close to the surface.

Paddlers may want to avoid certain lower sections (such as below the Homestead Dam) during the "thick" of Salmon season (most of September) to avoid conflicts with wading or on-shore anglers.

Although hook hazards (hanging from branches) and fish line hazards (hanging from branches and underwater) can be present along any part of any of the rivers (during any season), they are most likely on popular fishing sections of the Betsie River.

Type of bottom: Mostly sand, some silt and muck, and scattered areas of gravel and clay especially in the upper portion of the river downstream from Grass Lake Dam.

Fish typically caught: The Betsie River offers wonderful numbers of steelhead and chinook (king) and coho salmon during their spawning runs each year as they come in from Lake Michigan. The salmon run is from late August through late October and the steelhead run is later in the fall through early spring. These fine fish can get above the Homestead Dam to areas near Thompsonville, but a good percentage remain below M-115. The best salmon and steelhead fishing is below the Homestead Dam.

The Betsie River also offers a large population of resident brown and rainbow trout. For example, below Grass Lake

Dam, and above where the Little Betsie River joins in, expect some deep pools and excellent trout fishing. There's a fair fishery for browns from the Homestead Dam to Thompsonville. In the lower part of this river, browns larger that 20" have been caught.

There is an April through June run of white sucker as they come in from Lake Michigan.

Look for bluegill, largemouth bass, northern pike, rock bass, and smallmouth bass above Grass Lake Dam and below Homestead Dam.

At the Homestead Dam area there are reports of bluegill, brown trout, largemouth bass, perch, rainbow trout, rock bass, salmon, smallmouth bass, steelhead, and white sucker.

Access points: This three-day-long river has 20 points of access:

A. Green Lake — DNR boat launch
B. Betsie River Road Two-track
C. Grass Lake Dam — DNR access site
D. Wallin Road
E. Carmean Road
F. King Road
G. Wolf Road — DNR access site
H. Haze Road
I. Kurick Road
J. Psutka Road
K. County Line Road
L. Fred's Landing
M. Homestead Dam — DNR access site
N. US-31 — DNR access site
O. Grace Road — DNR access site
P. River Road (East) — DNR access site
Q. River Road (West) — DNR access site
R. Elberta Railroad Bridge
S. Betsie Lake/Elberta Marina
T. Betsie Lake/Frankfort Municipal Boat Launch

Details for each section:

- Betsie River Section A to B — Green Lake to the Betsie River Road Two-track
  - **Length**: 0.5 miles in Green Lake, 1.8 miles on the river.
  - **Paddle time**: 1.1 hours.
  - **Map**: goo.gl/maps/qVcbf
  - **Details**: Although Green Lake is out of the scope of this book, it's mentioned because it's the start of the navigable part of the river.

    Starting at the DNR boat launch on Green Lake, travel south 0.5 miles along the west shore of the lake to the entrance to the river. The slow-moving river flows through a wooded and wetland area.

    650 feet downriver from the lake is the Betsie River Road bridge At 1.2 miles Hall Creek enters on the left (south).
  - **Shuttle road:** Betsie River Road.

- Betsie River Section B to C — Betsie River Road Two-track to the Grass Lake Dam
  - **Length**: 3.1 miles.
  - **Paddle time**: 1.5 hours.
  - **Map**: goo.gl/maps/VGvH6
  - **Details**: Start at the "Betsie River Road Two-track" access if you want to avoid paddling in Green Lake. The river flows slowly through an open, marshy, and treeless area. Along the way:
    - 0.6 miles before the end of this section, Grass Lake Creek comes in on the right (northwest) from Grass Lake.
    - 0.4 miles before the end, Pickerel Creek enters the river on the left (southeast) from the Twin Lakes.

(Note that Grass Lake, Grass Lake Creek, Pickerel Creek, and the Twin Lakes are all covered later in this guide). On days with lighter winds it's also fairly easy to paddle **upstream** from the Grass Lake Dam most of the way to Green Lake.

- **Note:** With the building of the Grass Lake Dam, the water in the Betsie River above the dam, Grass Lake, Grass Lake Creek, Pickerel Creek, and the Twin Lakes was raised a few feet. This makes for easy traveling but there's no solid shore on any of these bodies of water. What might appear to be land is really a floating mat of loosely interwoven vegetation. So plan accordingly for lunch break, rest stops, etc.
- **Shuttle roads:** Grass Lake Dam, Reynolds, Cinder, Bendon, Rhodes, and Betsie River Roads.

- Betsie River Section C to D — Grass Lake Dam to Wallin Road
  - **Length**: 4.0 miles.
  - **Paddle time**: 1.6 hours.
  - **Map**: goo.gl/maps/fEoo
  - **Details**: The river passes under Reynolds Road bridge, a.k.a. the Woirol Bridge (at 2.6 miles), through the trestles of a former old railroad bridge (at 3.2 miles), under Nostwick Road bridge (a few hundred feet later), and under Wallin Road bridge (at 3.7 miles). The pull-out point is 0.3 miles (around 7 minutes) past Wallin Road bridge.

    Now below the dam the river picks up the pace compared to above the dam. Also, for the final third of this section (after the Reynolds Road bridge) the river runs a bit narrower and a faster than the two thirds above.
  - **Alerts**: Stay to the left at the **Reynolds Road bridge** for the best results.

When the water level is average or higher (such as during the spring and/or after a long rainy period), the clearance of the **Nostwick Bridge** can be quite low; in some cases, too low to paddle under and remain in your boat! So it is **highly recommended** to scout this bridge before starting your trip. When on the water, take care to make sure you and all those with you can make it easily under and through. There is NO easy portage here. Also, stay to the right here for the best results — the left side can be very shallow, both under the bridge and after. Location: **goo.gl/maps/i13tJ**

Also scout the **Wallin Road bridge**, as there can be logs piled up in front of the culverts. Note that before the bridge, the left channel of the river is not navigable, so the right channel must be used. As you'll see on-site, this can make things very tricky if the right-hand-side tube is blocked.

- **Shuttle roads:** Wallin, Reynolds, and Grass Lake Dam Roads.

- Betsie River Section D to E — Wallin Road to Carmean Road
  - **Length**: 2.4 miles.
  - **Paddle time**: About an hour.
  - **Map**: goo.gl/maps/BAZ1
  - **Details**: The river passes by the walls of the former Long Road bridge (at 0.4 miles) and under a private access bridge (at 2.1 miles) a few minutes before getting to the Carmean Road bridge.
  - **Shuttle roads:** Carmean and Wallin Roads.

- Betsie River Section E to F — Carmean Road to King Road
  - **Length**: 2.8 miles.
  - **Paddle time**: 1.2 hours.
  - **Map**: goo.gl/maps/STMBx

- o **Details**: The river passes under the Thompsonville Road bridge (at 2.2 miles) about 15 minutes before getting to the King Road bridge. There are very few houses or cottages along the way.
- o **Shuttle roads:** King and Carmean Roads.
- Betsie River Section F to G — King Road to Wolf Road
  - o **Length**: 1.5 miles.
  - o **Paddle time**: 0.6 hours.
  - o **Map**: goo.gl/maps/oXZR
  - o **Details**: The Little Betsie River joins the main Betsie River at the east one mile along the way. (Although several miles long, the Little Betsie is not large enough for any boats.) Much of this section passes through the area of the former containment pond for the Thompsonville power dam that was just beyond Wolf Road. You may also notice (or encounter) many deadheads (old-growth logs that never made it to the mill) stuck in the bottom but can lurk close to the surface. About 800 feet before the Wolf Road bridge the river passes under the former Ann Arbor Railroad bridge which is now used by the Betsie Valley Trail.
  - o **Shuttle roads:** Wolf and King Roads.
- Betsie River Section G to H — Wolf Road to Haze Road
  - o **Length**: 1.2 miles.
  - o **Paddle time**: 0.5 hours.
  - o **Map**: goo.gl/maps/Rgr4
  - o **Details**: A few hundred feet beyond Wolf Road bridge, there is now little evidence of the former Thompsonville power dam but a small rapids. Built in 1903, the dam failed in 1989 and was removed. But it helped make Thompsonville a viable concern and maintain the town's reputation for "the best-lit city in northern Michigan," established in the

1890s. This section is a beautiful wooded stretch, wild, no development, and runs a little deeper than the previous section.
- **Shuttle roads:** Haze, Lindy, 3rd Street, Gallagher, and Wolf Roads.

- Betsie River Section H to I — Haze Road to Kurick Road
  - **Length:** 4.3 miles.
  - **Paddle time:** Less than 2 hours.
  - **Map:** goo.gl/maps/8dTv
  - **Details:** There are occasional homes and cottages set back from the river, yet the area still maintains a wild character. The river passes under Lindy Road (at 3/4 of a mile) and M-115 (at 3.2 miles).
  - **Alert:** At Kurick Road there are four large, 185-feet-long **culverts.** July, 2014: only the far left culvert was passable, but easily done. The other three were blocked by logs piled up in front of them. It's **highly recommended** to scout these before starting your trip. Once on the water, always look through this (or any) culvert before entering to make sure it's clear, as rubble has been known to build up inside or just outside of the tubes. Be prepared to portage here, if need be. You can land on the left (south) side of the river.
  - **Shuttle roads:** Kurick, Weldon, Lindy and Haze Roads. Note that Weldon Road becomes Kurick Road on the south side of M-115.

- Betsie River Section I to J — Kurick Road to Psutka Road
  - **Length:** 4.3 miles.
  - **Paddle time:** Less than 2 hours.
  - **Map:** goo.gl/maps/ZYeG

- **Details**: There are several homes and cottages set back from the river along the first two-thirds, yet the area still maintains its wild character.
- **Shuttle roads:** Psutka, Dzuibanek, & Kurick Roads.

- Betsie River Section J to K — Psutka Road to County Line Road
  - **Length**: 2.9 miles.
  - **Paddle time**: 1.2 hours.
  - **Map**: goo.gl/maps/7GsX
  - **Details**: Another nice wooded stretch.
  - **Shuttle roads:** County Line and Psutka Roads.

- Betsie River Section K to L — County Line Road to Fred's Landing
  - **Length**: 9.7 miles.
  - **Paddle time**: About 4 hours.
  - **Map**: goo.gl/maps/Rw6j
  - **Details**: A long, pretty, but slightly more challenging section. At times there have been a few log jams to climb over or portage around (and note that these can happen along *any* section). There's a footbridge at Old King Road (at 6.3 miles). About 400 feet later Dair Creek joins the river on the right (east). At 7.0 miles the river passes under M-115 again. The better salmon fishing starts near the latter part of this section closer to the Homestead Dam.
  - **Shuttle roads:** Fred's Landing, Demerly, M-115, Dair Mill, King, Longstreet, and County Line Roads.

- Betsie River Section L to M — Fred's Landing to Homestead Dam
  - **Length**: 2.9 miles.
  - **Paddle time**: 1.2 hours.
  - **Map**: goo.gl/maps/447P

- o **Details**: The last third of this section is slower, wider, and can run shallow in some areas. This is where you'll find the salmon that just made it past the Homestead Dam.
- o **Shuttle roads:** Dam, Love, US-31, M-115, Demerly and Fred's Landing Roads.

- **Betsie River Section M to N — Homestead Dam to US-31**
  - o **Length**: 1.3 miles.
  - o **Paddle time**: 0.6 hours.
  - o **Map**: goo.gl/maps/wVY8
  - o **Details**: Since this section is just below the dam, there can be many folks fishing here during salmon runs. A common trip is to join this and the next two sections, going from Homestead Dam to River Road (East), making a nice two-hour paddle.
  - o **Shuttle roads:** US-31, Love, and Dam Roads.

- **Betsie River Section N to O — US-31 to Grace Road**
  - o **Length**: 1.5 miles.
  - o **Paddle time**: 0.6 hours.
  - o **Map**: goo.gl/maps/trQX
  - o **Details**: In the first part of this section there are some tight turns and twists, as well as tree-fall and logs (above and below water) to avoid that beginners will likely find challenging. Local liveries eventually cut a path in the debris, but be careful here early in the season, especially after a hard winter.
  - o **Shuttle roads:** Grace Road and US-31.

- **Betsie River Section O to P — Grace Road to River Road (East)**
  - o **Length**: 1.4 miles.

- **Paddle time**: 0.6 hours.
- **Map**: goo.gl/maps/9ZhL
- **Details**: Along this very pretty and twisty section Rice Creek joins the river (at 1.2 miles). The creek flows through a man-made pond that's part of a water-powered sawmill then exits the pond via a dam with a nice waterfall before entering the river.
- **Shuttle roads:** River Road, US-31, and Grace Road.

- Betsie River Section P to Q — River Road (East) to River Road (West)
    - **Length**: 3.5 miles.
    - **Paddle time**: 1.5 hours.
    - **Map**: goo.gl/maps/9PPc
    - **Details**: A very popular section, good for most skill levels. There are a few nice back-water areas. The Crystal Lake Outlet creek enters on the right (north) 1.3 miles of the way along. Normally, the creek can be paddled up only a few hundred feet, but as far as M-115 is possible during high water periods (typical in early spring).
    - **Alert:** At the River Road (East) bridge, use the left (west) culvert. The right (east) one takes you into a tricky situation forcing an immediate left turn that can be difficult given the currents involved.
    - **Shuttle road:** River Road.

- Betsie River Section Q to R — River Road (West) to Elberta Railroad Bridge
    - **Length**: 4.9 miles.
    - **Paddle time**: Around 2 hours.
    - **Map**: goo.gl/maps/74HcR
    - **Details**: This section is a little wider and slower and is mostly in the Betsie River State Game Refuge. The first two-thirds are in woods; the last third is

open wetland and the river splits into several channels. Keep to the main channel on the right.

- o **Shuttle road:** River Road.

- **Betsie River/Lake Section R to S — Elberta Railroad Bridge to Elberta Marina**
  - o **Length**: 0.3 to 0.8 miles depending on route taken.
  - o **Paddle time**: At least 15 minutes and likely more depending on route taken, water height, and if you have to get out of your boat.
  - o **Map**: goo.gl/maps/mk5G
  - o **Details**: The river passes under the former Ann Arbor Railroad bridge and soon after that the Lake Street (M-22) bridge.
  - o **Note:** During Lake Michigan's higher water periods the Elberta Marina is a potential alternate river-trip end-point. Even then, expect to have to paddle out into Betsie Lake 1000 feet and then back along its west shore to get to the marina. (For the shortest route, pull your boat much of the way along the left (south) lake shore then paddle the last portion to the marina.) The water can even be so high it's impossible to get under the Lake Street (M-22) bridge.

    On the other hand, when Lake Michigan is at its average or lower levels, Betsie Lake just north of the Lake Street (M-22) bridge is too shallow for any boats.

    So, except during high water periods, this section is not recommended as part of a river trip.
  - o **Shuttle roads:** Lake Street (M-22) and River Road.

- **Betsie Lake Section S to T — Elberta Marina to Frankfort Municipal Boat Launch**
  - o **Length**: 0.8 miles.
  - o **Paddle time**: About 30 minutes.

- **Map**: goo.gl/maps/C6dA
- **Details**: This section is in Betsie Lake (a.k.a. Frankfort Harbor and Betsie Bay) — see Betsie Lake in the INLAND LAKES section for more details. The water can be very shallow in the south end. To get out into Betsie Lake from the Elberta Marina, hug the west shore for 1000 feet to stay in a deep enough channel. Like the previous section, this is not recommended as part of a river trip except during high water periods
- **Note:** As Betsie Lake is also a harbor, it's used by many vessels — primarily larger boats going out to Lake Michigan, but also many charter fishing boats using the harbor's several marinas.
- **Shuttle roads:** Lake Street (M-22), Main, and 9th Streets.

Access point details:

A. Betsie River Access — Green Lake Launch

- **Details:** DNR boat launch, hard-surface ramp for up to medium-sized boats on a trailer, parking, restroom.
- **Note:** Only smaller boats, such as car-tops, canoes, and kayaks are appropriate for the river.
- **Map:** 44.598447, -85.79223; goo.gl/maps/ggVPN
- **Directions from Honor:** From the intersection of US-31 (Main Street) and Henry Street, take US-31 9.2 miles east to Bendon Road (which is called Lake Ann Road on the north). Turn right (south) and go 1 mile south to where it curves to the east and becomes Rhodes Road (a.k.a. Diamond Park Road). Go 1 mile east to Betsie River Road. Turn right (south) and follow it 2 miles south, 1 mile east, then 0.1 miles south to the boat launch entrance on the left (east) side of the road.
- **Directions from Karlin:** From the intersection of M-137 (Karlin Road) and Betsie River Road, take Betsie River Road northeast then north a total of 1.7 miles (crossing

over the Betsie River on the way) to the boat launch entrance on the right (east) side of the road.

B. Betsie River Road Two-track

- **Details:** Very shallow gravel and sand light-duty launch, very limited parking, no restroom.
- **Map:** 44.596139, -85.817288; goo.gl/maps/FSbPv
- **Directions from Honor:** From the intersection of US-31 (Main Street) and Henry Street, take US-31 9.2 miles east to Bendon Road (which is called Lake Ann Road on the north). Turn right (south) and go 1 mile south to where it curves to the east and becomes Rhodes Road (a.k.a. Diamond Park Road). Go 1 mile east to Betsie River Road. Turn right (south) and follow it 2 miles to where the road bends to the left (east). Look for the two-track (there's a "Seasonal Road" sign at the entrance) going straight (south) and take it 0.3 miles to the access.
- **Directions from Karlin:** From the intersection of M-137 (Karlin Road) and Betsie River Road, take Betsie River Road northeast, north, then west a total of 2.8 miles (crossing over the Betsie River on the way) to where Betsie River Road bends to the right (north). Look for the two-track (there's a "Seasonal Road" sign at the entrance) on the left (south) and take it 0.3 miles to the access.

C. Betsie River Access — Grass Lake Dam

- **Details:** Access is at the Grass Lake Campground. There's a gravel launch above the dam, carry-in access below the dam, restroom, and limited parking.
- **Easiest access:** Above-the-dam access is a few hundred feet above the dam at the east end of the campground road loop. Below-the-dam access is just a few feet below the dam. If you're portaging around the dam, there's a 400-foot path through the woods along the river from above to below the dam.

- **Map for above-the-dam access:**
  44.591622, -85.847086; goo.gl/maps/rBgjB
- **Map for below-the-dam access:**
  44.592119, -85.848399; goo.gl/maps/MYtPO
- **Directions from Honor:** From the intersection of US-31 (Main Street) and Henry Street, take US-31 8.2 miles east to Reynolds Road. Turn right (south) and go 2.0 miles to Cinder Road. Turn right (west) and go 0.2 miles to S. Reynolds Road. Turn left (south) and go about 2.9 miles to the unsigned Grass Lake Dam Road. Turn left (east) and go 0.4 miles to the campground. See "At the campground" below.
- **Directions from Thompsonville:** From the intersection of Lindy Road and Thompsonville Road (County Road 669), take Thompsonville Road 4 miles north to Wallin Road. Turn right (east) and go 3 miles to Reynolds Road. Turn left (north) and go 2.3 miles to the unsigned Grass Lake Dam Road. Turn right (east) and go 0.4 miles to the campground. See "At the campground" below.
- **At the campground:** Bear to the right following the campground road loop. At 0.1 miles along is the pavilion on the right (south) that marks the head of the short path to the dam and below-the-dam access. Go another 0.1 miles to the east end of the road loop for the above-the-dam access site on the right (south) side of the road.

D. Betsie River Access — Wallin Road

- **Details:** Access is at the end of a 0.2-mile-long two-track accessed from the southwest corner (south side of road, west side of river). There's carry-in access, limited parking, and no restroom. (There's also access at nearby Long Road (975 feet downriver), but it's so close to this access point it's not covered.)
- **Map:** 44.568146, -85.896531; goo.gl/maps/zu5uw

- **Directions from Thompsonville:** From the intersection of Lindy Road and Thompsonville Road (County Road 669), take Thompsonville Road 4 miles north to Wallin Road. Turn right (east) and go 2.2 miles to the two-track just before the Betsie River bridge on the right (south) side of the road. Turn right (south) and go 0.2 miles to a small turn-around and the river access point.

E. Betsie River Access — Carmean Road Bridge
- **Details:** Carry-in access, roadside parking, no restroom.
- **Easiest access:** Northwest corner down a short grassy hill.
- **Map:** 44.555409, -85.918261; goo.gl/maps/sgKe3
- **Directions from Thompsonville:** From the intersection of Lindy Road and Thompsonville Road (County Road 669), take Thompsonville Road 1.4 miles north to King Road. Turn right (east) and go 1 mile to Carmean Road. Turn left (north) and go 0.9 miles to the bridge.

F. Betsie River Access — King Road Bridge
- **Details:** Carry-in access, roadside parking, no restroom.
- **Easiest access:** Northeast corner.
- **Map:** 44.542259, -85.942354; goo.gl/maps/bq4cv
- **Directions from Thompsonville:** From the intersection of Lindy Road and Thompsonville Road (County Road 669), take Thompsonville Road 1.4 miles north to King Road. Turn left (west) and go 0.2 miles to the bridge.

G. Betsie River Access — Wolf Road Bridge
- **Details:** DNR access site, carry-in access, small launch platform, parking, restroom.
- **Easiest access:** Downstream (west) of bridge on the south side of the river down the 500-foot sidewalk. (Going down the short hill on the north side of the river just west of the bridge will also work for kayaks.)
- **Map:** 44.528621, -85.948875; goo.gl/maps/PIqhD

- **Directions from Thompsonville:** From the intersection of Lindy Road (County Road 602, a.k.a. Lincoln Street) and Thompsonville Road (County Road 669), take Lindy Road 0.3 miles west to 3rd Street. Turn right (north) and go 0.5 miles to Gallagher Road. Turn left (west) and go 0.1 miles to the parking lot on the left (southwest) side of the road. (FYI: where the road curves north it becomes Wolf Road.)

H. Betsie River Access — Haze Road

- **Details:** Carry-in access, roadside parking, no restroom. Note: there is no longer a bridge here, so approach this site from the south off of Lindy Road.
- **Easiest access:** Southeast or southwest corners.
- **Map:** 44.525061, -85.958903; goo.gl/maps/jRJa4
- **Directions from Thompsonville:** From the intersection of Lindy Road (County Road 602, a.k.a. Lincoln Street) and Thompsonville Road (County Road 669), take Lindy Road 1 mile west to Haze Road. Turn right (north) and go 0.3 miles to the river.

I. Betsie River Access — Kurick Road Land Bridge

- **Details:** Carry-in access, roadside parking, limited off-road parking a short distance away, no restroom.
- **Easiest access:** Southwest corner (south side of the river, west side of bridge, downstream of the culverts). From the road there's a sandy path down a mild slope to the river with a sandy and relatively shallow spot to launch/land your boat. (It is possible to access at the northwest corner, but the bank is high and the water deep so it's not recommended.)
- **Parking Details:** Park on Kurick Road south of the guardrail on the west side of the road. Better yet, park in the grassy area on the northwest corner. To get there — from the west side of Kurick Road north of the river at Dzuibanek Road, go west just 30 feet to the two-track on the south side of the road. Pull in there and park. To return to the "easiest access" spot

mentioned above, take the "goat paths" on the west slope of the land bridge or walk back via the roads.
- **Map:** 44.501521, -85.979491; goo.gl/maps/BAWvM
- **Directions from Thompsonville:** From the intersection of Thompsonville Road (County Road 669) and Lindy Road (County Road 602), take Lindy Road 2 miles west to Weldon Road (County Road 677). Turn left (south) and go 1.3 miles to the bridge. Note that Weldon Road becomes Kurick Road south of M-115.

J. Betsie River Access — Psutka Road Bridge
- **Details:** Carry-in access, roadside parking, no restroom.
- **Easiest access:** Southeast corner (on the upstream and left side of river)
- **Map:** 44.496162, -86.029948; goo.gl/maps/L3aOm
- **Directions from Thompsonville:** From the intersection of Thompsonville Road (County Road 669) and Lindy Road (County Road 602), take Lindy Road 2 miles west to Weldon Road (County Road 677). Turn left (south) and go 0.5 miles to County Line Road (a.k.a. Smeltzer Road). Turn right (west) and go 2.5 miles to Psutka Road. Turn left (south) and go 1.2 miles to the bridge. Note that Weldon Road becomes Kurick Road south of M-115.

K. Betsie River Access — County Line Road Bridge
- **Details:** Carry-in access, roadside parking, no restroom.
- **Easiest access:** Southeast corner.
- **Map:** 44.513923, -86.04403; goo.gl/maps/1ZY7x
- **Directions from Thompsonville:** From the intersection of Thompsonville Road (County Road 669) and Lindy Road (County Road 602), take Lindy Road 2 miles west to Weldon Road (County Road 677). Turn left (south) and go 0.5 miles to County Line Road (a.k.a. Smeltzer Road). Turn right (west) and go 3.2 miles to the bridge (just east of Moore Road). Note that Weldon Road becomes Kurick Road south of M-115.

L. **Betsie River Access — Fred's Landing**
- **Details:** Carry-in access, limited parking, no restroom. This road is not recommended for standard cars as it may occasionally be muddy, sandy, and have deep ruts. Vehicles with four-wheel-drive and/or higher ground clearance are recommended.
- **Map:** 44.578799, -86.052479; goo.gl/maps/SzyD6
- **Directions from Benzonia:** From the traffic light (westbound M-115 and US-31), take US-31 south 2.3 miles to eastbound M-115. Turn left (southeast) and go 1.6 miles to Demerly Road. Turn left (east) and go 0.3 miles to Fred's Landing Road. Turn left (north) and go about 1 mile down to the river.

M. **Betsie River Access — Homestead Dam**
- **Details:** DNR access site, carry-in access, parking, restroom.
- **Easiest access:** Access points to the river are a few hundred feet above and below the dam. If you're portaging around the dam, there are walkways for the 400-foot carry from above to below the dam.
- **Map for above-the-dam access:**
  44.596249, -86.07914; goo.gl/maps/HtQ39
- **Map for below-the-dam access:**
  44.596502, -86.080566; goo.gl/maps/ZwO7E
- **Directions from Benzonia:** From the traffic light (westbound M-115 and US-31), take US-31 0.9 miles south to Love Road (called Grace Road on the west side of US-31). Turn left (east) and go 1 mile to Dam Road. Turn right (south) and go 0.6 miles to the parking lot for the dam/access site.

N. **Betsie River Access — US-31**
- **Details:** DNR access site, carry-in access (down a 500-foot path on a hill), parking, restroom. Being so close to the Homestead Dam, many paddlers skip this access site and use Grace Road or River Road (East). During

salmon runs this can be a good place to start a river trip to avoid those fishing along the river upstream.

- **Map:** 44.600348, -86.096639; goo.gl/maps/XlXwo
- **Directions from Benzonia:** From the traffic light (westbound M-115 and US-31), take US-31 1.3 miles south to the access site's entrance on the left (east) side of the road.

O. Betsie River Access — Grace Road

- **Details:** DNR access site, carry-in access, parking, restroom.
- **Map:** 44.605657, -86.11289; goo.gl/maps/fPpib
- **Directions from Benzonia:** From the traffic light (westbound M-115 and US-31), take US-31 0.9 miles south to Grace Road (called Love Road on the east side of US-31). Turn right (west) and go 0.6 miles to the access site's entrance on the right (northwest) side of the road.

P. Betsie River Access — River Road (East)

- **Details:** DNR access site, carry-in access, limited parking, no restroom. This is sometimes called the Smith Bridge.
- **Map:** 44.617391, -86.122534; goo.gl/maps/u821V
- **Directions from Benzonia:** From the traffic light (westbound M-115 and US-31), take US-31 0.2 miles south to Traverse Avenue (called River Road west of Benzonia and all the way to M-22 near Elberta). Turn right (west) and go 1.1 miles to the access site's entrance on the left (south) side of the road.

Q. Betsie River Access — River Road (West)

- **Details:** DNR access site, concrete slab launch, parking, no restroom. This is sometimes called the Lewis Bridge.
- **Map:** 44.618951, -86.168269; goo.gl/maps/FA9jv
- **Directions from Benzonia:** From the traffic light (westbound M-115 west and US-31), take US-31 0.2

miles south to Traverse Avenue (which is called River Road west of Benzonia and all the way to M-22 near Elberta). Turn right (west) and go 3.3 miles to the entrance to the access site on the right (north) side of the road (which is just across the bridge and just west of Adams Road).

- **Directions from Frankfort:** From the intersection of Forest Avenue (M-115) and Lake Street (M-22), take Lake Street 0.9 miles south to River Road. Turn left (southeast) and go 2.7 miles to the entrance to the access site on the left (north) side of the road (which is just after Adams Road and just before the bridge).

R. **Betsie River/Lake Access — Elberta Railroad Bridge**

- **Details:** Carry-in access, roadside parking, no restroom. Once used by the Ann Arbor Railroad, the bridge is now used by the Betsie Valley Trail. When Lake Michigan is not at its higher levels, this is the recommended end-point for river trips because the south end of Betsie Lake can be extremely shallow near the Lake Street (M-22) bridge.
- **Easiest access:** From River Road, walk the 50-foot access path to the Betsie Valley Trail, turn right (west) and follow it for 400 feet to the bridge. The best access is on the south side of the bridge and east side of the river.
- **Map:** 44.619187, -86.220251; goo.gl/maps/bTvTs
- **Directions from Frankfort:** From the intersection of Forest Avenue (M-115) and Lake Street (M-22), take Lake Street 0.9 miles south to River Road. Turn left (southeast) and go 650 feet to the short access path to the Betsie Valley Trail on the right (south) side of the road.

S. **Betsie River/Lake Access — Elberta Marina**

- **Details:** Marina, municipal boat launch, gravel and hard-surface ramp, parking, no restroom.

- **Note:** This boat launch is not recommended for boats over 16 feet. During low water periods the marina can be very shallow and there can be logs obstructing easy travel. Also, the south end of Betsie Lake can be extremely shallow, especially near the Lake Street (M-22) bridge and when Lake Michigan is not at its higher levels. After going under the Lake Street bridge getting to the marina can be a real challenge. But, if you can get to it, there's a deeper channel along the west shore of Betsie Lake north of the marina for several hundred feet. Otherwise, it's highly recommended to end river trips at the Elberta Railroad Bridge. So, save the Elberta Marina (and Frankfort municipal boat launch) for exploring other parts of Betsie Lake. (See Betsie Lake in the INLAND LAKES section for more details.)
- **Map:** 44.619929, -86.225114; goo.gl/maps/ZdFMJ
- **Directions from Frankfort:** From the intersection of Forest Avenue (M-115) and Lake Street (M-22), take Lake Street 1.1 miles south then west (crossing over the Betsie River) to the entrance to the marina on the right (north) side of the road.

T. Betsie River/Lake Access — Frankfort Boat Launch

- **Details:** Municipal boat launch with a large, multiple-vehicle, hard-surface ramp which can accommodate larger trailerable watercraft. There's a fish-cleaning station, running water, parking, and restrooms. A user fee is required for this site. Since the northern part of Betsie Lake is also Frankfort Harbor, this launch is used primarily by boats going out to Lake Michigan. See Betsie Lake in INLAND LAKES section for more details.
- **Note:** This access site is not typically used as, or practical for, part of a river trip. The southern part of Betsie Lake can often be too shallow and there can be a lot of larger boat traffic on the northern part.
- **Map:** 44.631268, -86.230319; goo.gl/maps/puaFN

- **Directions from Frankfort:** From the intersection of Forest Avenue (M-115) and Lake Street (M-22), take Forest Avenue 0.4 miles west to 9th Street. Turn left (south) and go 1.5 blocks (crossing Main Street) to the boat launch.

PADDLE TIP: Never do a river trip alone, but always with at least one other boater. Make sure all boaters keep track of one another and stay within **hailing distance** of each other -- in case of trouble, or just the need to stop. And if you find yourself in potential trouble, don't hesitate or be shy -- call out! That way others can be ready assist you just in case.

---

2. Upper Platte River

General location: The river runs east to west in the central part of the county, east and west of Honor.

General description: The navigable portion of the Platte River is divided into two sections, the Upper and Lower; they are significantly different from each other and separated by the substantial Platte Lake. Most of the Upper Platte is clearer, faster, narrower, colder, and trickier to navigate than the Lower Platte or even the Betsie River. For the last two miles past Indian Hill Road (west of Honor) the river is wider, slower, and easier paddling. The river runs mostly through woods, yet there's some development (cottages and homes) around the town of Honor and in a few other scattered locations. It's a fun and beautiful river.

Major tributaries: Stanley (by way of Brundage), Brundage, Carter, and Collision Creeks, and the Deadstream (which is fed by Little Platte Lake, the North Branch Platte River, and a few smaller creeks).

Map of area: goo.gl/maps/JGVF

Map of river: atic.biz/water_maps/upper_platte_river.jpg

Length: 24 miles. But the navigable portion — from US-31 (east of Honor) to Deadstream Road — is only 9 miles long.

(This includes 0.4 miles of the Deadstream from the river to the Deadstream Road access point).

Paddle time: Navigable portion — US-31 (east of Honor) to Deadstream Road — 3 hours.

Depth: Perhaps an average of 1.5 feet with some scattered deep and quiet holes. Expect higher water in the spring and after heavy rains. A few scattered patches of the river can be less than 4 inches deep during hotter/drier summer months.

Width: 15 to 70 feet wide.

Type of water and difficulty: Faster, narrower river, generally not for beginners, but still Class I. There are plenty of obstacles to maneuver around as well as some shallower sections to navigate. Intermediate paddlers and above will enjoy this river and its surrounding wilderness. It is not recommended for novice paddlers unless they do not mind the potential of getting wet! Due to the many tight turns involved, this river is much easier to do in a shorter boat (such as a 9 to 12-foot kayak) than a 17-foot canoe. Significantly more than the Betsie River, the average gradient (drop) is 13 feet per mile.

Key obstructions: Being mostly in the woods, there can be "sweepers" — low-hanging branches that can "sweep" you from your boat. There is also plenty of tree-fall to maneuver around as well as other natural and man-made obstacles.

Type of bottom: Mostly sand, some areas of silt and gravel.

More details for the river: The river starts many miles to the east at Long Lake in Grand Traverse County and passes through Lake DuBonnet, Lake Ann, and Bronson Lake. It is not until below the fish hatchery (on US-31 east of Honor) that it becomes navigable.

Along this navigable portion the river passes under bridges at Haze Road (0.9 miles), Jean Lane, a.ka. Burris Bridge (1.9 miles), Pioneer Road (3.4 miles), South Street

(5.6 miles), Henry Street (5.9 miles) in Honor, US-31 west of Honor (6.6 miles), and Indian Hill Road (7.0 miles).

Alert: At South Street in Honor, use right tube to avoid a small rock dam on the left that's 30 feet past the bridge.

Although not an official access point, the river can be accessed from South Street north of the bridge on the east side of the road in the ditch by where the river first becomes parallel to the road. This is a handy end-point for those wanting a shorter trip (around 1.7 hours) on just the faster and mostly undeveloped part of the river.

Beyond US-31 (west of Honor) the river is a bit wider and slower making for easy paddling, and there's almost no development past Indian Hill Road — it's a nice wild area.

Near the end, about 1.7 miles past Indian Hill Road and very close to Platte Lake (which you will not be able to see), there's a "T" in the river. To the left is an 800-foot channel to Platte Lake — it can be impassable due to lots of tree-fall so it's not recommended. So turn right and in 300 feet the Deadstream enters the river on the right. (If for some reason you're going to Platte Lake, stay on the river and in 0.4 miles you'll be at the lake.) Otherwise, turn right and go up the very slow-moving Deadstream 0.4 miles to the Deadstream Road access site — it's on the right just before the road and the dam.

For more about the Deadstream and an alternate way into Little Platte Lake see "Deadstream" in the CREEKS section.

Fish typically caught: Expect coho and chinook salmon during their late summer/early fall spawning runs because the DNR always lets a decent percentage through the weir on the Lower Platte River. There's a steelhead run from November through April with the best fishing typically during the end of the run. White suckers have a run here from April through June. Throughout the year look for resident brown and rainbow trout. Near the end, from Indian Hill Road to Platte Lake, look for large migratory browns during their October runs. In fact, expect any species that populates the lake to be present in this section, in season.

More details for fishing: There are many riffles and runs, several deep holes in the outside of the turns, and scattered brush, rocks, and tree-fall in the river where you can expect to find fish lurking. The section from US-31 (East) to Honor is a designated Blue Ribbon Trout Stream.

More details for paddling: This river is appropriate for intermediate paddlers and above. Expect to navigate through narrow passages and around logjams, tree-fall, sweepers, shallow gravel bars, and other natural and man-made obstacles.

Access points:

A. US-31 (east) — DNR access site
B. Deadstream Road

Access point details:

A. Upper Platte River Access — US-31 (East)
- **Details:** DNR access site at Veteran's Park, carry-in access at the southwest corner, wooden platform, parking restroom.
- **Map:** 44.659336, -85.944027; goo.gl/maps/IgmyK
- **Directions from Honor:** From the intersection of US-31 (Main Street) and Henry Street, take US-31 3.8 miles east to Veteran's Park on the right (south) side of the road and just before the bridge over the river.

B. Upper Platte River Access — Deadstream Road
- **Details:** Carry-in access on the southeast corner, roadside parking, no restroom.
- **Map:** 44.683935, -86.059415; goo.gl/maps/HWu3N
- **Directions from Honor:** From the intersection of Main Street (US-31) and Henry Street, take Main Street 0.1 miles northwest to Deadstream Road (County Road 708). Bear to the right and go 2.3 miles watching for

where the Deadstream passes under the road. The river access point is just before that on the left (south) side of the road.

> **PADDLE TIP**: For river trips — **always prepare for getting wet**, taking on water, and the possibility completely dunking. This means dressing appropriately (such as no cotton), bringing along a change of clothes in a dry bag, putting loose gear in storage compartments or tied down, and making sure all gear is protected from getting wet or lost if you tip over.

3. Lower Platte River

General location: Northwestern area, northwest of Honor and Platte Lake.

General description: The Lower Platte River is the tamer of the two navigable Platte River sections. It's warmer, wider, and slower than the Upper Platte and likely the easiest river paddling in the county. It begins at the northwest corner Platte Lake, crosses under M-22, flows through Loon Lake, and eventually empties into Lake Michigan. There are a handful of cottages and homes along the river but it's mostly undeveloped and travels through woods and some open wetland. Most of the river, from before M-22 to Lake Michigan, is in the Sleeping Bear Dunes National Lakeshore.

Note: The use of any area in the Sleeping Bear Dunes National Lakeshore requires a national park pass.

Major contributors: Platte Lake, Mud Lake, Loon Lake

Map of area: goo.gl/maps/URWIq

Map of river: atic.biz/water_maps/lower_platte_river.jpg

Length: 4.6 miles. The distance traveled by boat will be different because of the access points involved.
- Platte Lake (Arborvitae Rd.) to Lake Michigan: 5.5 miles
- M-22 to landing site near the end: 4.1 miles
- Loon Lake launch to landing near the end: 3.1 miles

Paddle times:
- Platte Lake (Arborvitae Rd.) to Lake Michigan: 3 hours
- M-22 to landing site near the end: 2 hours
- Loon Lake launch to landing near the end: 1.5 hours

Depth: Perhaps an average of 2 feet with some scattered deep and quiet holes, some as much as 6 feet, and a few shallower areas where it's easy to run aground in hotter/drier months.

Width: 50 to 100 feet with a few narrower channels and a few wider areas.

Type of water and difficulty: Easy water and easy paddling for all skill levels. The gradient is just 3 feet per mile.

Key obstructions: Not many, just some occasional tree-fall at the sides of the river.

Type of bottom: Mostly sand, some silt.

Motors allowed: Yes, but it's a "no wake" river — any boat with a motor must not exceed a "slow--no wake" speed and there's a speed limit of 5 mph. Note that Loon Lake is a "no wake" lake, as well.

More details for the river: There's a lot of activity on this river during summer months; the kayak/canoe/tube livery on M-22 at the river does a lot of business. See "Details for each section" below for more paddling information.

At the end before the river empties into Lake Michigan, there are the following:
- Landing and loading areas for boats.
- Concrete boat ramp at the end of Lake Michigan Road.
- Lots of small dunes to play in.
- A very nice big sandy beach on Lake Michigan.
- A fun place to swim and float down the warmer river into the cooler Lake Michigan.
- Two parks: The Lake Township Park with a parking area, grassy park, and picnic tables. The rest of the area, parking, and restrooms are part of the Sleeping Bear Dunes National Lakeshore. There is a small fee to

use the Lake Township Park parking lot and the Lakeshore requires a national park pass.

Fish typically caught: Expect brown trout, largemouth bass, northern pike, rainbow trout, rock bass, smallmouth bass, and small panfish. Look for coho and chinook salmon during their late summer/ early fall runs. Note that the salmon are stopped at the weir; some are collected and some are let through. There's a steelhead run from November through April with the best fishing typically during the end of the run. White suckers have a run from April through June.

More details for fishing: There are some occasional deep holes on the outside of turns and scattered tree-fall at the sides of the river.

More details for paddling: When the salmon are running many of them will be encountered in the river — they will encounter your boat, too — especially just above the weir.

Access points:
A. Platte Lake Arborvitae Launch
B. M-22 Launch
C. Loon Lake Launch
D. El Dorado Launch
E. Lake Township Park Landing
F. Lake Michigan Road End Launch

Details for each section:

- Lower Platte River Section A to B — Platte Lake Arborvitae Launch to M-22 Launch
    o **Length**: 1.3 miles.
    o **Paddle time**: Less than an hour.
    o **Map**: goo.gl/maps/7esuc
    o **Details**: This section is for those who want to do ALL of the Lower Platte and don't mind paddling in a lake for a little while. Travel less than 0.9 miles along the west shore of Platte Lake to the beginning of the river, then 0.4 miles to just past

the M-22 bridge — the platform for the access site is on the right.
- **Shuttle roads:** Lake Michigan Road, M-22, Platte Road, Arborvitae Road.

- **Lower Platte River Section B to C — M-22 Launch to Loon Lake Launch**
  - **Length**: 1 mile.
  - **Paddle time**: Half an hour.
  - **Map**: goo.gl/maps/NybQV
  - **Details**: Include this section if you want to do most of the river but do not want to go on Platte Lake.

    About two-thirds of the way along on the right is the 600-foot creek going up to the pretty and wild 59-acre Mud Lake. Give it a try if the water is high enough. Early on there are a few fallen trees to maneuver around then the rest of the way is clear. See the INLAND LAKES section of this guide for more about Mud Lake — it is very aptly named.

    Where the river empties into Loon Lake it's very shallow and sandy. Often the far left side of the river is slightly deeper. Don't be surprised to have to exit your boat for a short way here. (For an alternate route, about 400 feet before the lake is a small channel on the right side that stays deep enough all the way out to the lake.)

    Once at the lake, if using Loon Lake Launch it's 600 feet to the left (south). If you're continuing on down the river, turn right at the lake and follow the shore about 0.5 miles to the northwest corner where the river continues.
  - **Shuttle roads:** M-22, Lake Michigan Road.

- **Lower Platte River Section C to D — Loon Lake Launch to El Dorado Launch**
  - **Length**: 1.9 miles.
  - **Paddle time**: About an hour.

- **Map**: goo.gl/maps/3fyLx
- **Details**: Some folks start their river trip here — it provides the easiest boat access, avoids the shallow area where the river enters the lake, yet cuts only half an hour off the travel time.

  On Loon Lake, follow the right-hand-side (east and northeast) shore for about 0.6 miles to the northwest corner of the lake where the river continues. Along the way, watch out for where the river enters the lake — move out from the shore a bit to avoid running aground. Once beyond the lake and on the river, about 0.6 miles from Loon Lake is the gate for the weir. It's open most of the time but in the early fall it's closed to harvest salmon. On the left (west) side of the river is a short and easy portage around the gate.
- **Shuttle roads:** Lake Michigan Road, M-22.

• Lower Platte River Section D to E — El Dorado Launch to Lake Township Park Landing
  - **Length**: 1.2 miles.
  - **Paddle time**: About 40 minutes.
  - **Map**: goo.gl/maps/0v52W
  - **Details**: Very squiggly but lots of fun. Expect to encounter a few wider and shallower areas where it's easy to run aground during lower water conditions. This is a common section for folks to float down on tubes during the summer.
  - **Shuttle road:** Lake Michigan Road.

• Lower Platte River Section E to F — Lake Township Park Landing to Lake Michigan Road End Launch
  - **Length**: 0.1 miles.
  - **Paddle time**: About 3 minutes.
  - **Map**: goo.gl/maps/kVRV3

- ○ **Details**: This short extension is used when exiting at the boat launch at the end of Lake Michigan Road. Where to end your trip mostly depends on where you parked and if you want to paddle out to Lake Michigan (800 feet downstream) and back.

Access point details:

A. Lower Platte River Access — Platte Lake Arborvitae Launch

- **Details:** DNR boat launch, hard-surface ramp for up to medium-sized boats on a trailer, short dock, parking, restroom. Start here to do ALL of the Lower Platte and don't mind traveling in a lake for a little while.
- **Note:** Only smaller boats such as car-tops, canoes, and kayaks are appropriate for doing the whole river.
- **Map:** 44.696167, -86.120718; goo.gl/maps/HQDpM
- **Directions from Honor:** From the intersection of US-31 (Main Street) and Henry Street, take US-31 1.3 miles west to Platte Road. Turn right (west) and go 4.4 miles to Arborvitae Road. Turn right (north) and go 0.2 miles to the public access on the right (east) side of the road.

B. Lower Platte River Access — M-22 Launch

- **Details:** Carry-in access, parking, restroom, inside the Sleeping Bear Dunes National Lakeshore. From the parking lot on Lake Michigan Road just north of M-22, there's a short sidewalk down to a wooden platform along the river. The Lower Platte's main kayak and canoe livery is just across the river and most of their customers start at this point.
- **Map:** 44.711588, -86.11932; goo.gl/maps/z3BJx
- **Directions from Honor:** From the intersection of Main Street (US-31) and Henry Street, take Main Street 0.1 miles northwest to Deadstream Road (County Road 708). Bear to the right and go 5.3 miles to M-22. Turn left (west) and go 0.6 miles to Lake Michigan Road. Turn right (north) and go 0.2 miles to the parking area for the access site.

C. **Lower Platte River Access — Loon Lake Launch**
- **Details:** Hard-surface boat ramp with dock, parking for vehicles with trailers, pavilion, picnic tables. restrooms, inside the Sleeping Bear Dunes National Lakeshore.
- **Map:** 44.708922, -86.126368; goo.gl/maps/VKG43
- **Directions from Honor:** From the intersection of Main Street (US-31) and Henry Street, take Main Street 0.1 miles northwest to Deadstream Road (County Road 708). Bear to the right and go 5.3 miles to M-22. Turn left (west) and go 1 mile to the entrance for the access site on the right (northwest) side of the road.

D. **Lower Platte River Access — El Dorado**
- **Details:** Hard-surface boat ramp, wooden platform, parking, restroom, inside the Sleeping Bear Dunes National Lakeshore.
- **Map:** 44.726558, -86.143481; goo.gl/maps/ivAM4
- **Directions from Honor:** From the intersection of Main Street (US-31) and Henry Street, take Main Street 0.1 miles northwest to Deadstream Road (County Road 708). Bear to the right and go 5.3 miles to M-22. Turn left (west) and go 0.6 miles to Lake Michigan Road. Turn right (north) and go 1.8 miles to the access site on the left (south) side of the road.

E. **Lower Platte River Access — Lake Township Park Landing**
- **Details:** Sand landing for small boats, carry-in access, parking, restrooms, picnic tables, sand dunes, beach, and the Lake Township Park. This is the end-point for local canoe and kayak liveries. The parking lot on the northeast side of the grass park is part of Lake Township and there is a small fee to park there. The rest of the area is part of the Sleeping Bear Dunes National Lakeshore and requires a national park pass.
- **Map:** 44.729853, -86.156437; goo.gl/maps/bkJD2

- **Directions from Honor:** From the intersection of Main Street (US-31) and Henry Street, take Main Street 0.1 miles northwest to Deadstream Road (County Road 708). Bear to the right and go 5.3 miles to M-22. Turn left (west) and go 0.6 miles to Lake Michigan Road. Turn right (north) and go 2.4 miles to the parking areas for the access site. The landing is in the southwest corner of this area just west of (behind) the restrooms.

F. Lower Platte River Access — Lake Michigan Road End Launch

- **Details:** Hard-surface boat ramp, parking, restrooms, picnic tables, sand dunes, beach, and the Lake Township Park. This is an alternate end-point for those doing a Platte River trip. The mouth of the Platte is just beyond this point. The parking lot on the northeast side of the park is part of Lake Township and there is a small fee to park there. The rest of the area is part of the Sleeping Bear Dunes National Lakeshore and requires a national park pass.
- **Map:** 44.730871, -86.15618; goo.gl/maps/Cb8Am
- **Directions from Honor:** From the intersection of Main Street (US-31) and Henry Street, take Main Street 0.1 miles northwest to Deadstream Road (County Road 708). Bear to the right and go 5.3 miles to M-22. Turn left (west) and go 0.6 miles to Lake Michigan Road. Turn right (north) and go 2.4 miles to the parking areas for the access site. The ramp is at the end of the road.

CREEKS

There are countless creeks in the county, many unnamed. Five of them are more like small rivers but their current is very mild and they can be easily paddled upstream as well as down. They are the Deadstream, Grass Lake Creek, Herring Creek, Otter Creek, and Pickerel Creek.

CREEKS at a GLANCE

Benzie County Creek	Navigable Length (miles)	Paddle Time, one-way (hours)	Average Depth (feet)	Width (feet)	Difficulty	Number of Access Points
1. Deadstream	1.1	1	2	25	Easy	1
2. Grass Lake Creek	0.7	0.3	2	40-70	Easy	1
3. Herring Creek	1.3	0.7	1.5	15-30	Easy	1
4. Otter Creek	2.0	1	1.2	25-50	Easy	1
5. Pickerel Creek	2.0	1.8	1.5	15-35	Easy	1

1. Deadstream

General location: Central area, northwest of Honor.

General description: Very slow-moving, nearly river-sized "stream" flowing from Little Platte Lake to the Upper Platte River just above (Big) Platte Lake. It has become known as the Deadstream, but technically it's the final portion of the North Branch Platte River whose channels flow into Little Platte Lake and this stream. It's surrounded mostly by wetland with some bits of woods. The dam on this stream at Deadstream Road maintains the depth of Little Platte Lake. This waterway can be used to access the Upper Platte River and Little Platte Lake.

Major contributors: Little Platte Lake, North Branch Platte River, and an unnamed creek — made up of many smaller streams combined — coming from the wetland area to the east.

Map of area: goo.gl/maps/HcCq

Map of creek: atic.biz/water_maps/deadstream.jpg

Length: 1.1 miles — 0.4 miles south of Deadstream Road and 0.7 miles north.

Paddle time: Depends on if you're paddling upstream or down. In total, it's less than an hour when paddling downstream from Little Platte Lake to the Upper Platte River.

Depth: An average of 2 feet. The upper section's depth is controlled by the dam at Deadstream Road.

Width: An average of 25 feet.

Type of water and difficulty: Slow-moving, nearly flat water and very easy paddling.

Key obstructions: None other than the dam at Deadstream Road which must be portaged to do the whole stream.

Type of bottom: Mostly sand, some organic and muck.

More details for the creek: From the Deadstream Road access point, there are two choices:
- travel downstream 0.4 miles to the Upper Platte River just before it enters Platte Lake.
- travel upstream 0.7 miles to Little Platte Lake.

Fish typically caught: There are lots of smaller fish like bluegill, largemouth bass, perch, and smallmouth bass, but this creek is generally not considered a great spot for fishing.

More details for paddling: The southern section of this creek is often used as the last leg of an Upper Platte River trip. It can also be used to go to Platte Lake via the river.

The northern section of this creek is used as alternate access to Little Platte Lake. Along the way you'll encounter:
- Fairly soon on the right (east) — an unnamed creek fed by many smaller streams in the wetland area to the east. You can paddle up this maybe 0.3 miles.
- Near the end, on the right (northeast) — one of the three final channels of the North Branch Platte River. You can paddle up this maybe a few hundred feet.

Access point: Deadstream Road.

- **Details:** Roadside parking, no restroom.
    - South side: Carry-in access on the southeast corner. This is the common end-point for those paddling the Upper Platte River.
    - North side: Carry-in access most easily done at a finger of the creek 120 feet to the east of where the main stream goes under the road.
- **Map for access to the north:**
  44.684171, -86.058946; goo.gl/maps/580vw
- **Map for access to the south:**
  44.683935, -86.059415; goo.gl/maps/HWu3N
- **Directions from Honor:** From the intersection of Main Street (US-31) and Henry Street, take Main Street 0.1 miles northwest to Deadstream Road (County Road 708). Bear to the right and go 2.3 miles watching for where the Deadstream passes under the road.

2. *Grass Lake Creek*

General location: Southeastern area, south of Bendon.

General description: Short, slow-moving creek, with a lot of aquatic growth. It flows from Grass Lake to the Betsie River and is surrounded by open wetland. This creek is the only public access to Grass Lake.

Major contributors: Grass Lake

Map of area: goo.gl/maps/nWI88

Map of creek: atic.biz/water_maps/grass_lake_creek.jpg

Length: 0.7 miles from the Betsie River to Grass Lake. Add another 0.6 miles for access to the creek via the Betsie River above Grass Lake Dam.

Paddle time: 40 minutes total paddling upstream on the Betsie River and Grass Lake Creek from the Grass Lake Dam to Grass Lake. The return time should be less as you're traveling downstream.

Depth: Perhaps an average of 2 feet, but there are some nice deep holes along the way.

Width: 40 to 70 feet.

Type of water and difficulty: Slow-moving creek, easily paddled. Later in the summer there are plenty of lily pads and other aquatic growth that could slow you down, but there's a narrow open channel allowing you to easily get through.

Key features/obstructions: The aquatic growth might be considered both a feature and an obstruction.

Also, with the building of the Grass Lake Dam, the water in the Betsie River above the dam, Grass Lake, Pickerel Creek, and the Twin Lakes was raised a few feet. That makes for fairly easy traveling, but there's no solid ground along the shore on any of these bodies of water, so plan accordingly for lunch break, rest stops, etc.

Type of bottom: Sand, organic, and silt.

More details for the creek: The only public access to Grass Lake is via the Betsie River and this creek. (Grass Lake is covered in the INLAND LAKES section of this guide.) Note that it's a fairly open area so it can be windy.

Fish typically caught: There is likely bluegill, largemouth bass, northern pike, perch, rock bass, and smallmouth bass, but generally this creek is not considered a great spot for fishing.

Access point: Grass Lake Campground above the Dam

- **Details**: DNR access site at the Grass Lake Campground, gravel launch above the dam, limited parking restroom.

- **Easiest access**: Above-the-dam access is a few hundred feet past the dam at the end of the campground road loop.

- **Map**: 44.591622, -85.847086; goo.gl/maps/rBgjB

- **Directions from Honor:** From the intersection of US-31 (Main Street) and Henry Street, take US-31 8.2 miles east to Reynolds Road. Turn right (south) and go 2.0 miles south to Cinder Road. Turn right (west) and go 0.2 miles to S. Reynolds Road. Turn left (south) and go about 2.9 miles to the unsigned Grass Lake Dam Road. Turn left (east) and go 0.4 miles to the campground. Bear to the right and go less than 0.2 miles to the east end of the campground road loop. The launch is on the right (south) side of the road.

- **Directions from Thompsonville:** From the intersection of Lindy Road and Thompsonville Road (County Road 669), take Thompsonville Road 4 miles north to Wallin Road. Turn right (east) and go 3 miles to Reynolds Road. Turn left (north) and go 2.3 miles to the unsigned Grass Lake Dam Road. Turn right (east) and go 0.4 miles to the campground. Bear to the right and go less than 0.2 miles to the east end of the campground road loop. The launch is on the right (south) side of the road.

3. Herring Creek

General location: Southwestern area, south of Elberta.

General description: Fairly slow moving creek flowing from Upper to Lower Herring Lake. The navigable section is from Upper Herring Lake to M-22. It travels through woods and wetland and is almost all wild.

Major contributors: Upper Herring Lake

Map of area: goo.gl/maps/38GY

Map of creek: atic.biz/water_maps/herring_creek.jpg

Length: 1.3 miles one-way, Upper Herring Lake to M-22.

Paddle time: 40 minutes downstream, but it's close to 2 hours round trip.

Depth: Perhaps an average of 1.5 feet.

Width: 15 to 30 feet wide.

Type of water and difficulty: Winding yet slow-moving creek, easily paddled. Coming back upstream is a little more work than paddling downstream, of course.

Key obstructions: A few bits of old docks and tree-fall along the way.

Type of bottom: Mostly sand, some silt.

More details for the creek: Technically the creek starts in the wetlands east of Upper Herring Lake, but that portion is usually not navigable. The usable part starts via the DNR boat launch on Upper Herring Lake. From there go west 500 feet to the start of the creek. About half-way along is a very small pond on the right (north), accessible during higher water periods. It can be fairly dense with lily pads and aquatic growth. Although the creek flows past M-22 (to Lower Herring Lake), you cannot get very far past M-22, so it's best to turn around before the M-22 bridge. Also, the last few hundred feet of the creek before M-22 gets very narrow, perhaps 10 feet wide. Longer kayaks will have a hard time turning around, so it's best to do so before that section. And, be sure to save some energy for the return trip paddling upstream.

Fish typically caught: There are lots of smaller fish like bluegill, largemouth bass, perch, and smallmouth bass, but generally this creek is not considered a great spot for fishing.

Access point: Upper Herring Lake DNR Boat Launch

- **Details**: Hard-surface ramp for up to medium-sized boats on a trailer, short dock, restroom, parking for a few vehicles with trailers and a few without. The water at the launch area can be very shallow, in which case a motor cannot be used until several yards from shore. There's also a lot of rushes here but with an open channel through them.
- **Note:** Only smaller boats such as car-tops, canoes, and kayaks are appropriate for the creek.
- **Map:** 44.570676, -86.185789; goo.gl/maps/iCRpQ
- **Directions from Frankfort:** From the intersection of M-115 (Forest Avenue) and M-22 (Lake Street), take M-22 4.5 miles south to Herron Road. Turn left (east) and go 1.2 miles to the launch site's access road on the right (south).

PADDLE TIP: Look for the **main channel** — often you'll want to follow this, but not ALL the time!

For the kinds of rivers in northern Michigan, there is usually a main channel flowing within the river. It can be down the center as one might expect, but often it will weave from side to side, and on turns it usually runs along the outside. The main channel can often be spotted by a string of bubbles and a faster current moving within the river. In the main channel the water runs deeper and faster; out of it the water is shallower and slower.

Be aware, however, that on sharp turns the main channel can sweep you right into obstructions, such as those fallen from the nearby shore. Always look ahead and prepare well ahead of time to avoid any obstacles — both in the water and above it.

When rivers widen out they usually also get shallower, making following the main channel even more of a necessity to avoid running aground.

4. Otter Creek

General location: Northwestern corner, north of Honor.

General description: Gentle stream flowing from Otter Lake to Lake Michigan surrounded by open wetland and woods in the Sleeping Bear Dunes National Lakeshore. Due to being partially spring and stream-fed this water is much cooler than nearby small lakes and the Lower Platte River.

Note: The use of any area in the Sleeping Bear Dunes National Lakeshore requires a national park pass.

Major contributors: Otter Lake and several springs and streams coming in from surrounding woods and hills.

Map of area: goo.gl/maps/74IE

Map of creek: atic.biz/water_maps/otter_creek.jpg

Length: Two miles in total from Otter Lake to Lake Michigan. (Near Lake Michigan's shore, the creek often goes several hundred feet paralleling the shore before entering the lake.) The distance one can travel by boat varies based on the depth but it's typically 1.6 miles from the Aral Road bridge upstream to about 1000 feet north of Otter Lake.

Paddle time: A little over 2 hours round trip.

Depth: It varies, but there's a nice "main" channel ranging from 8 inches to a few feet deep that runs along the western shore much of the way, then closer to the (southern) end the deepest channel can vary from side to side to down the middle.

Width: 25 to 50 feet wide with several wider patches, one that's a few hundred feet.

Type of water and difficulty: Winding yet gentle flowing water and easy paddled. Just look for and follow the deeper main channel.

Key obstructions: Shallow bottom, some tree-fall.

Type of bottom: Sand, organic, marl, and muck.

More details for the creek: This creek is best done in kayaks.

From Aral Road to Lake Michigan there is too much tree-fall in the creek to be suitable for boats. The navigable portion starts at Aral Road then goes upstream to just north of Otter Lake.

For the first few hundred feet there are submerged planks along the shore which were used during the days of the sawmill at the nearby historic village of Aral.

Note that the creek splits apart at times and there are streams coming in from the east confusing the issue. Just follow the main channel covered in the **Depth** section above.

You cannot get all the way to Otter Lake because its small outlet is impassable and travels partially "underground." It does not become navigable until joining with other streams about 1000 feet north of Otter Lake, which is the southern end of your paddle trip.

This is a wonderful and wild marsh and woods area to explore — no people and lots of water fowl, animal life, and myriad plant life. It's terrific for photographers, bird watchers, and other wildlife enthusiasts. In just one visit many ducks, several kingfishers, a few egrets, two bald eagles, a sand hill crane, a blue heron, and a green heron were spotted.

Fish typically caught: There are lots of smaller fish like bluegill, largemouth bass, perch, and smallmouth bass, but generally this creek is not considered a great spot for fishing.

Access point: Aral Road.

- **Details:** Carry-in access. There's roadside parking on Aral Road north of the creek or back along Esch Road where there's a restroom and access to Lake Michigan. Put in on the north side of the creek about 12 feet east of the bridge. Stay off the other river banks.

- **Map:** 44.761658, -86.07391; goo.gl/maps/LUxIM
- **Directions from Honor:** From the intersection of Main Street (US-31) and Henry Street, take Main Street 0.1 miles northwest to Deadstream Road (County Road 708). Bear to the right and go 0.9 miles to Indian Hill Road. Turn right (north) and go 6.3 miles to Esch Road. Turn left (west) and go 1.2 miles to Aral Road. Turn left (south) and go 400 feet to Otter Creek.

5. Pickerel Creek

General location: Southeastern area, south of Bendon.

General description: Slow-moving creek flowing from the Twin Lakes to the Betsie River just above the Grass Lake Dam. Surrounded mostly by open wetland and backed by some woods, it's a wonderful, wild, unspoiled area.

Major contributors: Twin and Upper Twin Lakes

Map of area: goo.gl/maps/nREY

Map of creek: atic.biz/water_maps/pickerel_creek.jpg

Length: About 2 miles. Add another 0.4 miles for access to the creek via the Betsie River from just above Grass Lake Dam. Add another 0.7 miles for exploring the lakes at the top and their inlet to the east.

Paddle time: 3.5 hours round trip. Add more time if you plan on visiting the lakes at the top and their inlet.

Depth: Perhaps 1.5 feet average with some deeper holes and several shallower patches.

Width: 15 to 35 feet wide.

Type of water and difficulty: Winding, slow-moving, nearly flat water and very easy paddling, even upstream. Just look for and follow the deeper main channel.

Key feature/concern: With the building of the Grass Lake Dam, the water in the Betsie River above the dam, Grass Lake, Grass Lake Creek, Pickerel Creek, and the Twin Lakes was raised a few feet. This makes for easy traveling but there's no solid ground along the shore on any of these bodies of water. What might appear to be land is really a floating mat of loosely interwoven vegetation. So plan accordingly for lunch break, rest stops, etc.

Key obstructions: There is plenty of plant life in the creek in late summer/early fall, but there's an easy channel through it most of the way. There can be a bit of tree-fall, and there are two beaver dams to climb/slide over. Local residents try to keep these from being too built up so it's likely you can just "scootch" over them. After the second beaver dam it's only about 10 minutes to Twin Lake.

Type of bottom: Organic, sand, and muck.

More details for the creek: This creek is best done in kayaks. Start on the Betsie River at the Grass Lake Dam, travel 0.4 miles east and stay to the right. Watch for Pickerel Creek entering on the right, somewhat hidden behind an island. The creek starts out and ends wide but has some narrower sections along the way. When you get to the first lake (Twin Lake), travel to its east side where there's the 0.2-mile-long channel connecting to Upper Twin Lake. Pickerel Creek is the only public access to these lakes (which are covered in the INLAND LAKES section). Upper Pickerel Creek flows into Twin Lake and is covered there, as well.

Fish typically caught: Bluegill, largemouth bass, northern pike, perch, rock bass, and smallmouth bass.

Where fish are typically found: Game fish of any decent size are found in the deeper regions, such as by Twin Lake.

Access point: Grass Lake Campground above the Dam

- **Details:** DNR access site at the Grass Lake Campground, gravel launch above the dam, restroom, limited parking.
- **Easiest access:** Above-the-dam access is a few hundred feet above the dam at the east end of the campground road loop.

- **Map:** 44.591622, -85.847086; goo.gl/maps/rBgjB

- **Directions from Honor:** From the intersection of US-31 (Main Street) and Henry Street, take US-31 8.2 miles east to Reynolds Road. Turn right (south) and go 2.0 miles south to Cinder Road. Turn right (west) and go 0.2 miles to S. Reynolds Road. Turn left (south) and go about 2.9 miles to the unsigned Grass Lake Dam Road. Turn left (east) and go 0.4 miles to the campground. Bear to the right and go less than 0.2 miles to the east end of the campground road loop. The launch is on the right (south) side of the road.

- **Directions from Thompsonville:** From the intersection of Lindy Road and Thompsonville Road (County Road 669), take Thompsonville Road 4 miles north to Wallin Road. Turn right (east) and go 3 miles to Reynolds Road. Turn left (north) and go 2.3 miles to the unsigned Grass Lake Dam Road. Turn right (east) and go 0.4 miles to the campground. Bear to the right and go less than 0.2 miles to the east end of the campground road loop. The launch is on the right (south) side of the road.

INLAND LAKES

There are 58 named inland lakes in Benzie County. Older maps show even more that have since dried up. There are several unnamed lakes, as well, most of which are very small and have no (easy) access. Many of the 58 are surrounded by private land with no public access. But 32 lakes in the county ARE publicly and easily accessible and covered in this guide. For most, access is via public access sites, but a few lakes can be entered only via connecting creeks. The 32 lakes range in size from 4 to 10,000 acres and are covered in the table and pages that follow.

Of the 32 lakes, 16 allow motors, 8 are "no wake" lakes, and 8 allow no motors, or a motor would not be practical. A "no wake" lake means any boat with a motor must not exceed a "slow--no wake" speed. The National Park Service adds a speed limit of 5 mph; in this guide that applies only to Loon Lake and the Lower Platte River.

In case you're wondering, the 26 lakes NOT covered are: Bell, Black, Bryan, Courson, Eliza, Hartman, Harvey, Holden, Hooker, Horseshoe, Lake Louise, Lake View, Lost, Lower Woodcock, Parsons, Peanut, Pigeon, Pikes, Ransom, Rush, Shavenaugh, Shorter, Sweet, Tarnwood, Upper Woodcock, and Wiltz. Also not covered is Bellows Lake east of Lake Ann. Even though a tiny western portion of it is in Benzie County, it's mostly in Grand Traverse County.

And a reminder (and repeat) — in the prevention of the spread of fish diseases and nuisance species, properly "cleaning boats, trailers, and other equipment between fishing trips to prevent transporting undesirable fish pathogens and organisms from one water body to another" is the most important step. Remember that Michigan law prohibits placing a boat, trailer, or other boating equipment into Michigan waters with any plant material attached. See this Web page for more information:

Preventing the spread of fish diseases and nuisance species
michigan.gov/dnr/0,1607,7-153-10364-160949--,00.html

INLAND LAKES at a GLANCE

Benzie County Lake	Area (acres)	Depth (feet)	Shoreline (miles)	Motors Allowed / Practical
1. Bass Lake	20	15+	1.0	no
2. Betsie Lake	289	0.3 - 30	3.0	No Wake
3. Bronson Lake	46	38	1.2	No Wake
4. Brooks Lake	21	33	0.8	YES
5. Cook Lake	4	15	0.35	no
6. Crystal Lake	9854	165	20.8	YES
7. Davis Lake	34	40	1.0	YES
8. Deer Lake	4	8+	0.4	no
9. Fuller Lake	12	24	0.7	No Wake
10. Garey Lake	28	33	0.9	YES
11. Grass Lake	105	4	2.2	YES
12. Herendeene Lake	37	37	1.1	No Wake
13. Lake Ann	527	76	6.1	YES
14. Lime Lake	15	25	0.8	YES
15. Little Platte Lake	820	7	6.2	YES
16. Long Lake	328	18	3.9	YES
17. Loon Lake	95	66	1.8	No Wake
18. Lower Herring Lake	450	60	3.8	YES
19. Mary's Lake	7	25	0.4	YES
20. Mud Lake (off of Lake Ann)	30	5+	1.4	YES
21. Mud Lake (near the Lower Platte River)	59	< 2	1.2	no
22. Mud Lake (off of Sanford Lake)	12	10+	0.5	No Wake
23. Otter Lake	64	15+	1.4	no
24. Pearl Lake	350	15+	7.6	YES
25. Platte Lake	2516	90	9.1	YES
26. Round Lake	15	6+	0.7	no
27. Sanford Lake	50	20+	1.6	No Wake
28. Stevens Lake	45	57	1.2	No Wake
29. Turtle Lake	38	22	1.4	YES
30, 31. Twin and Upper Twin Lakes	16 / 16	15+ / 8+	0.7 / 0.7	no / no
32. Upper Herring Lake	565	26	4.1	YES

1. Bass Lake

General location: Northwestern corner, north of Honor.

General description: A beautiful little lake in the Sleeping Bear Dunes National Lakeshore, just right for fishing or paddling. It's surrounded by woods and small hills with only one cottage left on the lake.

Note: The use of any area in the Sleeping Bear Dunes National Lakeshore requires a national park pass.

Map of area: goo.gl/maps/AlkYf

Lake area: 20 acres   **Shoreline length:** 1.0 miles

Lake depth: 15+ feet (likely at least 30 feet), deep for its size.

Type of bottom: Sand and muck.

Inlet: There's a very short inlet in the southeast corner connecting this lake to Deer Lake — unfortunately it can no longer be paddled.

Outlet: In the east part of a notch in the northwestern area of the lake is an outlet that flows into Otter Lake.

Key obstructions: Watch for logs and fallen trees all around the edges.

Motors allowed: No.

Fish typically caught: Bluegill, largemouth bass, northern pike, perch, rock bass, and smallmouth bass.

More details for fishing: The lake drops off fast and reaches a good depth quickly around all its edges. Logs and fallen trees all around the lake provide lots of good fish habitat.

Access point: Trails End Road

- **Details:** Short crushed-gravel path to a concrete brick launch, carry-in access only, dock with platform and bench, small parking area, restroom.

- **Map:** 44.736235, -86.065358; goo.gl/maps/f5Fhd
- **Directions from Honor:** From the intersection of Main Street (US-31) and Henry Street, take Main Street 0.1 miles northwest to Deadstream Road (County Road 708). Bear to the right and go 0.9 miles to Indian Hill Road. Turn right (north) and go 4.5 miles to Trails End Road. Turn left (west) and go 0.5 miles to an "S" turn in M-22. Go straight (west) on M-22 just over 0.1 miles to the west part of Trails End Road. Keep going straight (west) and follow the road 0.9 miles through a right then a left turn to the parking lot for the access site.

> **FISH TIP:** Did you know that the Michigan Department of Natural Resources' Fisheries Division does not receive any general fund tax dollars to support its activities? It depends heavily on angler dollars collected through fishing license sales and federal excise tax dollars from the sale of fishing tackle. That's why **buying a fishing license is so beneficial** to supporting the health of Michigan's fishing industry and prized freshwater fisheries. Fishing license dollars fund a variety of activities including: fish management work on the state's waters, habitat rehabilitation and protection, fish stocking, information distribution, education and outreach efforts to anglers and the public, and much more. *(Source: Michigan DNR)*

2. Betsie Lake (a.k.a. Betsie Bay)

General location: Western central area between Frankfort and Elberta.

General description: The northern portion of Betsie Lake is also known as Betsie Bay and Frankfort Harbor. It's open to Lake Michigan via a man-made channel at the west end. Once a natural harbor, this lake/bay has been developed since the 1800s, was home to the Ann Arbor car ferry fleet, and is now used for many purposes. The village of Elberta resides along the southwest side and the city of Frankfort on the north side. There are several marinas on the bay as well as the Frankfort Municipal Boat Launch so at times there can be numerous boats coming and going to Lake Michigan. The mouth of the Betsie River is at the southeast corner of the lake.

This lake is only occasionally fished by boat and explored by paddlers. The county's other inland lakes and waterways are usually preferred.

Map of area: goo.gl/maps/Rqfio

Lake area: 289 acres   **Shoreline length:** 3.0 miles

Lake depth: Perhaps an average of 5 feet. But the depth has a large range, from over 15 feet deep in the harbor area at the northwest, to 3 to 10 feet in the middle area, to as little as a few inches in the southeast. The depth varies based on the current height of Lake Michigan.

Type of bottom: Silt and mud.

Inlet: The Betsie River enters at the lake's southeast corner.

Outlet: There's a man-made channel out to Lake Michigan at the west end — it's part of Frankfort Harbor

Key features: This body of water has many uses and with that comes many features such as the "mud flats" at the south, several marinas, two fishing docks, shipping "bone yard", former car ferry docks, harbor, and channel out to Lake Michigan.

Key obstructions: The southern area of this lake during anything but high water periods is much too shallow for any boats. There is old timber near the shore around the old car ferry docks and rip-rap at the south shore of the bay's western section.

Motors allowed: Yes, but it's a "no wake" lake.

More details for the lake: Anyone on the lake should be very aware of all the boat traffic that can be present.

During Lake Michigan's higher water periods it's possible to travel through the southeast area of the lake, under the M-22 bridge, past the old railroad bridge, and into the wetland area of the Betsie River (where it splits into many channels).

During Lake Michigan's lower water periods it's not possible to travel even near the M-22 bridge. At times it's so shallow even the salmon have trouble getting past this area to get upstream.

Fish typically caught: Bluegill, brown trout, channel catfish, largemouth bass, northern pike, perch, rock bass, smallmouth bass, and walleye. White sucker during their runs in April through June. Coho and chinook salmon and steelhead during their annual spawning runs.

Where fish are typically found: Those who fish here by boat often do so as an extension of fishing in Lake Michigan; they troll from the big lake's channel to the Frankfort boat launch. A popular location is the more than 30-foot-hole on the south side of the west end of the harbor near the old car ferry docks.

Access points:

A. Elberta Marina
B. Frankfort Boat Launch
C. Betsie River

Access point details:

A. Betsie Lake Access — Elberta Marina

- **Details**: Marina, municipal boat launch, parking, no restroom. The ramp is mostly hard-surface with gravel near the water.
- **Note:** This launch is not recommended for boats over 16 feet. During low water periods the marina can be very shallow and there can be logs obstructing easy travel. Also, the southern portion of Betsie Lake can be extremely shallow, especially near the Lake Street (M-22) bridge and when Lake Michigan is not at its higher levels. Getting to and from the marina can be a challenge unless you stay in the deeper channel along the west shore of the lake and north of the marina for several hundred feet.
- **Map:** 44.619929, -86.225114; goo.gl/maps/ZdFMJ

- **Directions from Frankfort:** From the intersection of Forest Avenue (M-115) and Lake Street (M-22), take Lake Street 1.1 miles south then west (crossing over the Betsie River) to the entrance to the marina on the right (north) side of the road.

B. Betsie Lake Access — Frankfort Boat Launch

- **Details:** Municipal boat launch with a large, multiple-vehicle, hard-surface ramp which can accommodate larger trailerable watercraft. There's a fish-cleaning station, running water, parking, and restrooms. A user fee is required for this site. The launch is used primarily by boats going out to Lake Michigan.
- **Map:** 44.631268, -86.230319; goo.gl/maps/puaFN
- **Directions from Frankfort:** From the intersection of Forest Avenue (M-115) and Lake Street (M-22), take Forest Avenue 0.4 miles west to 9th Street. Turn left (south) and go 1.5 blocks (crossing Main Street) to the boat launch.

C. Betsie Lake Access — Betsie River

- **Details:** Access by boat via the Betsie River, such as from the Elberta Railroad Bridge. Doing so is often not very practical or possible as the water can be too shallow where the river empties into the lake.
- **Map:** 44.619187, -86.220251; goo.gl/maps/bTvTs
- **Directions to access:** See "Betsie River/Lake Access — Elberta Railroad Bridge" in the RIVERS section.

3. Bronson Lake

General location: Eastern central area, southwest of Lake Ann village.

General description: Nice, quiet lake just right for exploring. It's protected from the wind by the surrounding hills and trees that go down to the waterline. Except for a few homes and cottages on the west side, it's wild and undeveloped. The Platte River flows through the lake.

Map of area: goo.gl/maps/tJPS1

Lake area: 46 acres   **Shoreline length:** 1.2 miles

Lake depth: 38 feet in the center of the southern half, quite deep for its size. Around the west, south, and east sides there's a nice drop-off to 20 feet not too far from shore.

Type of bottom: Gravel, marl, organic, and sand.

Inlets: In the northeast corner a short stream comes in from the nearby 8-acre Hooker Lake. The Platte River enters the lake near the northern tip.

Outlet: At the southwest corner the Platte River flows out of the lake. About 700 feet down there's a log dam (part of an old beaver dam) which helps out by adding at least a few inches to the lake's depth.

Motors allowed: Yes, but it's a "no wake" lake.

Fish typically caught: Bluegill, crappie, largemouth bass, northern pike, perch, and rock bass.

More details for fishing: All around the lake there's lots of good fish habitat as well as interesting structure ranging from the steep/deep west side to the shallow north end.

More details for paddling: You can paddle part way up the short inlet coming from Hooker Lake, but getting to the lake is not easy — expect logs to go over and/or under and a small beaver dam to climb across.

Going up the Platte River north of the lake you can get about 1000 feet before encountering lots of tree-fall across the river.

Paddling down the Platte River southwest of the lake you can go about 700 feet downstream to a log dam. This wider part of the river is easy to paddle and has lots of aquatic undergrowth. (Entering the river on the left and 30 feet before the dam is a creek coming from Bell Lake).

Access point: Oakley Road.

- **Details:** Sand/gravel boat launch, very limited parking, no restroom. The 250-foot, loose-gravel road down to the launch is quite steep so a four-wheel-drive vehicle is highly recommended.
- **Map:** 44.690787, -85.88241; goo.gl/maps/twBrK
- **Directions from Honor:** From the intersection of US-31 (Main Street) and Henry Street, take US-31 4.3 miles east to Maple City Highway (County Road 669). Turn left (north) and go 2.0 miles to Bowers Road. Turn right (east) and go 0.5 miles to Oakley Road. Turn right (east) and go 1.3 miles to Jeri Road. Go straight (east) down the short and steep access road to the boat launch.

> FISH TIP: Expect good populations of both **largemouth** and **smallmouth bass** throughout Michigan. Largemouth, with lateral lines along their side, are typically found in shallower, warmer, and weedier water. Smallmouth, with vertical bars along their sides, are usually found in cooler, cleaner water and gravel or rocky habitat. But both types can be caught in the same bodies of water and often from the same general areas. *(Main source: Michigan DNR)*

4. Brooks Lake

General location: Northeastern area, northwest of Lake Ann village.

General description: Pretty and quiet smaller lake nestled in low hills and woods. Except for a few cottages it's wild all the way around.

Map of area: goo.gl/maps/CLfv7

DNR map: atic.biz/water_maps/brooks_lake.pdf

Lake area: 21 acres   **Shoreline length:** 0.8 miles

Lake depth: 33 feet near the center, quite deep for its size. The northwestern area and southeastern tip can be very shallow.

Type of bottom: Mostly organic, some sand around the edges.

Inlets and outlets: None.   **Motors allowed:** Yes.

Fish typically caught: Bluegill, crappie, largemouth bass, perch, other types of panfish, as well as reports of occasional brook trout, northern pike, and rainbow trout.

More details for fishing: There are some rushes around the shoreline, reeds at the northwest, and lily pads at the southeast. A quiet little lake and a good place to start for those new to fishing.

Access point: Brooks Lake Road.

- **Details:** DNR access site, gravel boat launch, restroom, limited parking.
- **Map:** 44.77139, -85.913204; goo.gl/maps/5qXAv
- **Directions from Lake Ann:** From the intersection of County Road 610 (Maple Street) and 1st Street, take County Road 610 west 3.2 miles to Maple City Highway. (Along the way, at 1.7 miles you'll curve right (north) on Ole White Drive, then at 2.2 miles you'll turn left (west) on Almira Road.) At Maple City Highway (County Road 669) turn right (north) and go 3.0 miles to Oviatt Road (a.k.a. Pettengill Road and County Line Road). Turn left (west) and go 0.8 miles to Brooks Lake Road. Turn left (south) and go 0.4 miles to the boat launch access road on the right (southwest) side of the road. The boat launch is less than 0.1 miles down this road.

5. Cook Lake

General location: Northeastern corner, north of Lake Ann village.

General description: Cute, quiet, and deep little lake, surrounded by woods and low rolling hills. There's no development — it's wild all around and straddles the Benzie/Leelanau County line.

Map of area: goo.gl/maps/JGWL8

Lake area: 4 acres   **Shoreline length:** 0.35 miles

Lake depth: 15 feet in the center, very deep for its size.

Type of bottom: Sand, clay, organic.

Inlets and outlets: None.   **Motors allowed:** No.

More details for the lake: This lake ties with Deer Lake for the smallest lake in the county, at least of named lakes with public access. Despite its size, its value is not diminished for fishing and aesthetic appeal.

Fish typically caught: Bluegill, crappie, largemouth bass, perch, and rock bass.

More details for fishing: There are plenty of reeds and some lily pads around the shoreline for fish habitat.

Access point: Lake Ann Road.

- **Details:** 200-foot sandy path to a sand launch, carry-in access only, limited parking, no restroom.
- **Map:** 44.776083, -85.834158; goo.gl/maps/Csc2k
- **Directions from Lake Ann:** From the intersection of Maple Street (County Road 610) and 1st Street, take Maple Street 0.3 miles east to (northbound) Lake Ann Road. Turn left (north) and go 3.3 miles to Davis Lake Road. Here the road turns to gravel and dirt two-track. Continue northeast then north on Lake Ann Road going 0.3 miles to the open parking area at the lake's northwest corner.

6. Crystal Lake

General location: Western central area, northeast of Frankfort, and northwest of Beulah.

General description: The largest inland lake in Benzie County (and the ninth largest in Michigan), this beautiful, clear, creek and spring-fed, sand-bottom (around the shores) jewel has many attractive qualities. It's surrounded by hills and woods but developed all around the shoreline — mostly with summer homes and cottages. There are also a few small resorts sprinkled about and the quaint village of Beulah (once known as Crystal City) at the east end. With its beautiful water and surroundings, this is one of the most sought-after locations in the area.

Map of area: goo.gl/maps/g4ILI

DNR map: atic.biz/water_maps/crystal_lake.pdf

Lake area: 9854 acres   **Shoreline length:** 20.8 miles

Lake depth: Lake experts say it's 165 feet deep, maps claim 175, and some local fishermen claim even more. Maps put the deepest area at the center of the lake. Much of the western half of the lake is 160 feet deep down the middle.

Type of bottom: Sand, gravel, marl, and muck.
- Sand — around all the shore, in most cases to depths of 20 feet, but as far out as 90 feet along much the middle of the south side off Mollineaux Bay.
- Gravel — found around all the shore out to depths of 10 to 20 feet.
- Marl — predominant in deeper water and the central area of the eastern fifth of the lake.
- Muck — found mostly just off the Cold Creek inlet at the east end of the lake.

Inlets: The major contributor is Cold Creek in the east end at Beulah Beach. The lake is also fed by 13 creeks and many near-shore and underwater springs. One of the creeks is the Round Lake Creek from Round Lake on the north side and enters at Herdman's Bay. (Round Lake is the only lake that feeds Crystal Lake and is a former bay from before Crystal was lowered about 20 feet in 1873.)

Outlet: There's an outlet with a dam on the south side in Mollineaux Bay — it flows south and connects to the Betsie River.

Motors allowed: Yes.

More details for the lake: Motor boats, water skiers, jet skis, pontoon boats, sailboats, the occasional regatta, kayaks, paddle boards, and swimmers are all common on the lake in the summer. But rarely are there ever many boats on the lake at one time. Look for fishing boats in spring, summer, and fall, and ice fishermen in mid to late winter.

Side note: Although rarely seen and protected by the state, there are lake sturgeon in Crystal Lake. There are sightings of these bottom-feeders being at least 6 feet long. They can grow even bigger and live to be 100 years old. Along with lake trout and whitefish, lake sturgeon are native to Crystal Lake and have inhabited it since at least the last ice age. Some say lake sturgeon are among the most primitive of fish and first appeared when land on Earth was still a single continent.

Fish typically caught: Rainbow and lake trout are stocked here each year. So expect rainbow trout, some big lake trout, and plenty of rock bass and smallmouth bass. Also present are bluegill, brown trout, burbot, cisco, coho salmon, lake whitefish, northern pike, perch, smelt, and white sucker.

Side note: The DNR says, "Perhaps the smallest of fish pursued by Michigan anglers — rainbow smelt — were planted in Crystal Lake in 1912 and they made their way into Lake Michigan. Crystal Lake was once one of the best-known hook-and-line smelt fisheries."

> **FISH TIP: Lake trout** prefer cold water and are often found at significant depths, though they can be taken in relatively shallow water in the spring and fall. They spawn in the fall, often on shoals and reefs. With the increasing presence of zebra mussels and the subsequent change in water clarity, lake trout behavior is changing and some are now being taken well up in the water column, often just below the surface. Crystal Lake in Benzie County is one of the better-known lake trout inland lakes in the state. *(Source: Michigan DNR)*

> **FISH TIP: Lake whitefish** are an important component to Great Lakes commercial fisheries and are becoming increasingly popular with recreational anglers in both the Great Lakes and inland waters. These fish make excellent table fare and put up a real tussle on the hook with a fight that resembles a rodeo bronco. Inland whitefish are most commonly associated with deep, clear-water lakes where they are targeted on or near the bottom. Generally, lakes with lake trout populations will also support lake whitefish. *(Source: Michigan DNR)*

Where fish are typically found: Look for rainbow trout off the eastern shore near and around the Beulah public boat launch. Look for smallmouths around the shores, such as the weed beds off of Beulah. Expect rock bass, panfish and northern pike in the weed beds on the east end of the lake and around rocky and gravelly areas. Expect good perch fishing in 20 to 30 feet of water around drop-offs. Find coho salmon, lake trout, brown trout, and rainbow trout at 70 feet plus, such as in the depths of the western half of the lake. In depths of 80 to 125 feet off of Railroad Point is prized lake trout location. At one time there was a run of smelt each April at Cold Creek.

More details for fishing: Some of the best fish ever eaten have been caught in this very clean water claim some long-time fishermen. There are not a lot of weeds in this lake, but expect a moderate amount of weed beds and vegetation above the drop-offs, and some weed beds off of Cold Creek.

More details for paddling: This large lake has many paddling uses, such as sea kayaking all around the lake or quiet sunset paddles along the shore on a calm evening.

Access points: Crystal Lake has seven main public access sites (as well as several minor road-end accesses):

A. Beulah Public Boat Launch & Beach
B. Fair Park in Beulah
C. Crystal Lake Boating Access Site
D. Crystal Lake Outlet
E. Lobb Road
F. Frankfort Public Beach & Boat Launch
G. North Shore Public Access Site

Access point details:

A. Crystal Lake Access — Beulah Public Boat Launch and Beach

- **Details:** Hard-surface boat ramp with docks, 3-block-long public beach, mouth of Cold Creek, nearby park, picnic tables, restrooms, pavilion, and basic parking (but none for vehicles with trailers).
- **Map:** 44.630136, -86.09564; goo.gl/maps/4Q2dP
- **Directions from Beulah:** From downtown (South Benzie Blvd), go west one block to Lake Street on Prospect Ave, Commercial Ave, or Clark Street. The boat ramp is at the west end of Clark Street (near the north end of the beach).

B. Crystal Lake Access — Fair Park in Beulah

- **Details:** Small park with sand boat launch, carry-in access only, no beach, picnic table, seasonal port-a-pottie, very limited parking.
- **Map:** 44.62754, -86.10156; goo.gl/maps/lImJB
- **Directions from Beulah:** From the five-corner intersection (S. Benzie Blvd, Spring Valley, Crystal Ave, and Prospect Ave), take Crystal Avenue 0.25 miles west

to the "Stop" sign at Benzie Street. The park is on the right (north) side of the road.

C. Crystal Lake Access — Crystal Lake Boating Access Site

- **Details:** Large DNR access site, multi-slot hard-surface boat ramp and docks, lots of parking, restrooms. Parking is 149 steps up the hill from the launch. East of the parking area is a self-service boat washing station — please use it to protect the lake from harmful invasive plant and animal species.
- **Map:** 44.63654,-86.12721; goo.gl/maps/2jlRK
- **Directions from Benzonia:** From the traffic light (westbound M-115 and US-31), take M-115 west 1.8 miles to Mollineaux Road. Turn right (north) and go just 300 feet to the entrance to the access site on the right (north) side of the road.

D. Crystal Lake Access — Crystal Lake Outlet

- **Details:** Dam and outlet for Crystal Lake, carry-in access only, wide but shallow beach area along the Betsie Valley Trail, very limited parking, no restroom.
- **Map:** 44.63676, -86.146944; goo.gl/maps/9Z7Pj
- **Directions from Benzonia:** From the traffic light (westbound M-115 and US-31), take M-115 west 1.8 miles to Mollineaux Road. Turn right (north) and go 1.0 mile to the small parking lot for the access site on the right (north) side of the road. It's immediately east of where the Betsie Valley Trail crosses the road and 130 feet east of where the outlet goes under the road.

E. Crystal Lake Access — Lobb Road

- **Details:** Popular yet very simple paved road-end boat launch with a few concrete blocks at the edge, roadside parking for only a few vehicles with trailers, no restroom. This site is appropriate only for smaller boats on trailers or carry-in access.
- **Map:** 44.653847, -86.185632; goo.gl/maps/RuKV8

- **Directions from Frankfort:** From the intersection of M-115 (a.k.a. Forest Avenue and Frankfort Hwy) and Lake Street (M-22), go east 1.0 mile on M-115 to Lobb Road. Turn left (north) and go 2.0 miles to S. Shore Drive on Crystal Lake. The boat launch is right there on the northeast side of the road.

F. Crystal Lake Access — Frankfort Public Boat Launch and Beach

- **Details:** Light-duty, very shallow boat launch — gravel driveway to metal grids on the sand near and in the lake, short dock, park, designated swimming area, 200-foot beach, picnic tables, swings, grill, pavilion, restrooms, parking, a.k.a. as Bellows Park.
- **Map:** 44.66100, -86.23204; goo.gl/maps/4yJpO
- **Directions from Frankfort:** From the intersection of 7th Street and Forest Avenue, go north on 7th Street 0.1 miles and bear to the left (northwest) — you're now on Crystal Ave. Go just under 0.1 miles to the west fork of Bellows Ave. Turn right (northeast) and go just under 0.1 miles to the main Bellows Ave. Veer left (north) and go 1.6 miles to S. Shore Drive on Crystal Lake. The boat launch and beach are at the northeast corner of this intersection. The park is on the southeast corner.

G. Crystal Lake Access — North Shore Public Access Site

- **Details:** Light-duty paved and concrete block boat launch, parking on the north side of Crystal Drive, no restroom. This is a popular launch site for smaller boats on trailers. It's also a five-acre county park sometimes known as Zada Price County Park, Mitchell Park, and the Wilson Property.
- **Map:** 44.647419, -86.095081; goo.gl/maps/3yyG5
- **Directions from Beulah:** From the five-corner intersection (S. Benzie Blvd, Spring Valley, Crystal Ave, and Prospect Ave), take Benzie Blvd 0.5 miles north to US-31 (Michigan Ave), Turn left (north) and go 0.4

miles to Crystal Drive. Turn left (north) and go 0.8 miles around to the north side of Crystal Lake. The boat launch is on the left (south) and parking is on the right (north) side of the road.

> FISH TIP: The **black crappie** found in Benzie County are most often associated with clear-water lakes. Shallow-water cuts and canals, especially those with dark bottoms (which warm faster than the main lake) are the first places to look for spring crappie. Similarly, crappie move into marinas or other protected coves. In rivers look for them in quiet waters away from the main current or below barriers where their upstream migration is impeded. *(Source: Michigan DNR)*

7. Davis Lake

General location: Near the northeastern corner, north of Lake Ann village.

General description: Pretty, smaller, clear-water lake sheltered from the wind by the surrounding gentle hills and woods. This tear-drop-shaped lake has about 15 homes/cottages sprinkled around it and straddles the Benzie/Leelanau County line.

Map of area: goo.gl/maps/PaXHO

DNR map: atic.biz/water_maps/davis_lake.pdf

Lake area: 34 acres   **Shoreline length:** 1.0 mile

Lake depth: 40 feet in the center, quite deep for its size. There are nice drop-offs around most of the shore. The change in depth from shore to the lake's center is fairly quick and consistent around most of the lake; in the northwestern tip the change is more gradual.

Type of bottom: Mostly organic, some sand and gravel around the shore.

Inlets and outlets: None.   **Motors allowed:** Yes.

Fish typically caught: Bluegill, largemouth bass, northern pike, perch, and rock bass. There are reports of occasional rainbow trout, as well. Expect decent size bass and bluegills, but smaller "hammer-handle" pike.

More details for fishing: There are scattered areas of rushes around the shoreline and some lily pads in the northwestern tip, otherwise it's pretty clear.

Access point: Davis Lake Road.

- **Details:** DNR access site, 100 feet wide, sand/gravel launch, tiny beach area, limited parking, restroom.
- **Map:** 44.775632, -85.860356; goo.gl/maps/vI8uL
- **Directions from Lake Ann:** From the intersection of Maple Street (County Road 610) and 1st Street, take Maple Street 0.7 miles west to (northbound) Reynolds Road (County Road 667). Turn right (north) and go 3.5 miles to Davis Lake Road. Turn left (west) and go 0.2 miles to the access road for the site. Turn right (west) and go 300 feet to access site.

8. Deer Lake

General location: Near the northwestern corner, north of Honor.

General description: Wild, quiet, and pretty little lake tucked away in the woods with some small hills to the west. There's no development on the lake and it's in the Sleeping Bear Dunes National Lakeshore.

Note: The use of any area in the Sleeping Bear Dunes National Lakeshore requires a national park pass.

Map of area: goo.gl/maps/2NnlL

Lake area: 4 acres   **Shoreline length:** 0.4 miles

Lake depth: 8+ feet (likely 15 feet), fairly deep for its size.

Type of bottom: Sand, muck, and organic.

Inlets: None.

Outlet: There's an outlet to Bass Lake on the northeast corner. It was once more open, now there's too much plant life and tree-fall to be able to paddle through.

Key obstructions: Logs & fallen trees all around the edges.

Motors allowed: No.

More details for the lake: This lake ties with Cook Lake for the smallest lake in the county, at least of named lakes with public access. Despite its size, its value is not diminished for fishing and aesthetic appeal.

Fish typically caught: Bluegill, largemouth bass, perch, northern pike, rock bass, and smallmouth bass.

More details for fishing: Like its neighbor just to the north (Bass Lake), the lake's depth drops off fairly fast around the edges. There are logs, fallen trees, and aquatic vegetation all around offering lots of good fish habitat.

Access point: Deer Lake Road.

- **Details:** Carry-in access only down a 100-foot path to the lake, parking for three vehicles at the most, no restroom. Four-wheel-drive is not required but does not hurt for traveling on Deer Lake Road; it starts out a full gravel road but soon becomes a narrow two-track.
- **Map:** 44.731627, -86.063439; goo.gl/maps/P1zVP
- **Directions from Honor:** From the intersection of Main Street (US-31) and Henry Street, take Main Street 0.1 miles northwest to Deadstream Road (County Road 708). Bear to the right and go 0.9 miles to Indian Hill Road. Turn right (north) and go 4.5 miles to Trails End Road. Turn left (west) and go 0.5 miles to an "S" turn in M-22. Go straight (west) on M-22 just over 0.1 miles to the west part of Trails End Road. Keep going straight (west) and follow the road 0.5 miles through a right then a left turn to the unsigned gravel road on the left (south) side of the road — this is Deer Lake Road. Turn left (south) and go 0.5 miles (going past Bass Lake) to the northeast corner of the lake. There's a rough 100-foot path to the lake.

> FISH TIP: **Brown trout** — though often thought of as denizens of Up North, these fish are more tolerant of warmer water than other trout species and have become the principle target of anglers in many rivers and streams across Michigan. In streams, browns (especially larger ones) seem to be photo-sensitive and are usually more cooperative on rainy or overcast days. They're sometimes found after a good rain in turbid river water. Browns are a favorite of fly fishermen, many of whom pursue them after dark during notable insect hatches, especially the giant Michigan mayfly. Brown trout also provide good fishing in many northern Michigan inland lakes. In the Lake Michigan and connected nearby water these trout are often taken in conjunction with coho in the spring or incidentally with other salmon during the summer. *(Source: Michigan DNR)*

9. Fuller Lake

General location: Northeastern area, northwest of Lake Ann village.

General description: Fairly secluded and quiet, smaller lake, accessed from Herendeene Lake. There's only one cottage on the lake, it's surrounded mostly by woods, and there's a golf course on the southwest side.

Map of area: goo.gl/maps/IWUHY

DNR map: atic.biz/water_maps/fuller_lake.pdf

Lake area: 12 acres   **Shoreline length:** 0.7 miles

Lake depth: 24 feet in the southwestern half, quite deep for its size.

Type of bottom: Organic.

Inlet: There's an inlet channel from Herendeene Lake on the upper southeast side.

Outlet: There's an outlet creek on the lower southeast side.

Key features: There's a marshy wetland section off the middle of the northwest side.

Key obstructions: There are some stumps scattered around the shoreline — created presumably when the lake was raised by the dam at the old mill.

Motors allowed: Yes, but it's a "no wake" lake.

More details for the lake: The outlet creek feeds a mill pond immediately to the south. It's believed the dam at the old mill on Hawks Road raised the lake at least a few feet and created the mill pond. The pond and dam are still present south of the lake.

Fish typically caught: Bluegill, crappie, largemouth bass, perch, and rock bass.

More details for fishing: There are some rushes and a fair amount of lily pads around the shoreline.

Access point: Outlet channel from Herendeene Lake.

- **Details:** The only access is via a short and narrow outlet channel from the west side of Herendeene Lake. It's only 1 foot deep and there's lots of aquatic plant life and some stumps to avoid.
- **Map:** 44.741213, -85.865707; goo.gl/maps/PjHCJ
- **Directions to access:** See access for Herendeene Lake.

10. Garey Lake

General location: Northeastern area, northwest of Lake Ann village.

General description: Another pretty little lake surrounded by woods and a few low hills. Except for a handful of cottages on the north side, it's wild all around. Woods come to the shore all around the lake, and there are a lot of older dead trees around the edge. The lake accessed via the Garey Lake Trail Camp and is also known as Gerry Lake.

Map of area: goo.gl/maps/prHXT

DNR map: atic.biz/water_maps/garey_lake.pdf

Lake area: 28 acres **Shoreline length:** 0.9 miles

Lake depth: 33 feet in the center, quite deep for its size. The drop-off from shore is gradual all around the lake.

Type of bottom: There's hard sand bottom with layer of organic material around the edges for much of the lake, otherwise the bottom is organic.

Inlets: At the eastern tip are two creeks, one connecting to Courson Lake to the northeast and another to an unnamed nearly-dry lake to the southeast.

Outlets: None. **Motors allowed:** Yes.

More details for the lake: The lake level rose in height at some point many years ago killing a lot of trees around the edge, so there are lots of older dead trees all around the lake both in and out of the water. There are two weed "islands" at the southwest, out a little way from the shore.

Fish typically caught: Bluegill, crappie, largemouth bass, northern pike, perch, and rock bass.

More details for fishing: Around the shoreline are several areas of rushes, lily pads, dead trees, fallen trees, logs, and branches — all offering some nice fish habitat. The water is not as clear as many other lakes in the county.

Access point: Garey Lake Trail Camp

- **Details:** Sand/gravel launch, parking away from launch site (in areas where there are no campsites), restroom. A Michigan Recreational Passport is required to use the area. The Shore-to-Shore horse trail passes through and uses this camp.
- **Map:** 44.77676, -85.937454; goo.gl/maps/iPBsc
- **Directions from Lake Ann:** From the intersection of County Road 610 (Maple Street) and 1st Street, take County Road 610 west 3.2 miles to Maple City Highway. (Along the way, at 1.7 miles you'll curve right (north) on Ole White Drive, then at 2.2 miles you'll turn left (west) on Almira Road.) At Maple City Highway

(County Road 669) turn right (north) and go 3.0 miles to Oviatt Road (a.k.a. Pettengill Road and County Line Road). Turn left (west) and go 2.1 miles to the entrance to the trail camp on the left (south) side of the road. The boat launch is about 0.2 miles to the southeast.

11. Grass Lake

General location: Southeastern area, south of Bendon.

General description: A wide open lake, completely wild all around with no development (other than a few old duck blinds). In late summer it lives up to its name with lots of sparse grassy areas throughout the lake. It's surrounded by wetland then backed by woods.

Map of area: goo.gl/maps/vqnEm

Lake area: 105 acres   **Shoreline length:** 2.2 miles

Lake depth: 4 feet, quite shallow for its size.

Type of bottom: Organic.

Inlets: There are inlet creeks on the northwest and northeast sides. At one time the Betsie River also flowed into the lake at the southeast corner.

Outlet: There's an outlet (Grass Lake Creek) to the Betsie River at the southern end; it's covered in the CREEKS section.

Key feature/concern: With the building of the Grass Lake Dam, the water in the Betsie River above the dam, Grass Lake Creek, Grass Lake, Pickerel Creek, and the Twin Lakes was raised a few feet. That makes for fairly easy traveling, but there's no solid ground along the shore on any of these bodies of water. What might appear to be land is really a floating mat of loosely interwoven vegetation. So plan accordingly for lunch break, rest stops, etc.

Key obstructions: There's lots of underwater plant life and scattered grass patches throughout the lake, but it's sparse enough for easy traveling. With no nearby trees around the lake it can be windy out on the lake.

Motors allowed: Yes, if you dare. But it's likely that in summer and early fall, there's too much plant life in Grass Lake Creek and the lake itself to make a motor practical. Perhaps in the spring a small motor could be safely used.

More details for the lake: The small island encountered when first entering the lake (with a duck blind on it) is rather unusual — it's a floating island. It's like the shore, a mat of loosely interwoven vegetation.

Fish typically caught: Smaller largemouth bass and northern pike, reports of bluegill and perch, but generally this lake not considered a great one for fishing.

Access point: The only access is via Grass Lake Creek off of the Betsie River above Grass Lake Dam. See the access to Grass Lake Creek in the CREEKS section for details.

12. Herendeene Lake

General location: Northeastern area, northwest of Lake Ann village.

General description: Lovely, clear-water, smaller lake with hills to the north and east and woods all the way around to the water's edge. Except for a few cottages and a tiny resort on the east side, it's otherwise undeveloped. There's access to Fuller Lake via the outlet channel to the west.

Map of area: goo.gl/maps/INYEe

DNR map: atic.biz/water_maps/herendeene_lake.pdf

Lake area: 37 acres   **Shoreline length:** 1.1 miles

Lake depth: 37 feet in the center of the eastern half, quite deep for its size. There's a 24-foot hole in the center of the western half.

Type of bottom: Marl, sand, and organic.

Inlet: There's a creek (which passes under the county's only covered bridge) coming in at the northeastern corner from an unnamed lake to the north.

Outlet: There's a short outlet channel at the west providing access to Fuller Lake.

Key obstructions: There are some stumps scattered around the shoreline — created presumably when the lake was raised by the dam at the old mill.

Motors allowed: Yes, but it's a "no wake" lake.

More details for the lake: It's believed the lake was raised at least a few feet by the dam at the old mill on Hawks Road, a short way to the southwest. Via the short outlet channel to the west is the only public access to Fuller Lake (a.k.a. "the back lake").

Fish typically caught: Bluegill, crappie, largemouth bass, perch, and rock bass.

Where fish are typically found: Look for crappies at the lake's two holes near the center of the eastern and western halves.

More details for fishing: The lake is protected from the wind by surrounding hills and woods. In summer there's a fair amount of rushes and lily pads around the shore.

Access point: Reynolds Road.

- **Details:** DNR access site, gravel launch, limited parking, restroom.
- **Map:** 44.740375, -85.858309, goo.gl/maps/rhMdu
- **Directions from Lake Ann:** From the intersection of Maple Street (County Road 610) and 1st Street, take Maple Street 0.7 miles west to (northbound) Reynolds Road (County Road 667). Turn right (north) and go 1.0 mile to the access road for the site. Turn left (west) and go 0.1 miles to the access site.

13. Lake Ann

General location: Northeastern area, southwest of Lake Ann village.

General description: Also known as Ann Lake, this is the fifth largest lake in the county. There's scattered development around the lake, mostly just cottages, but also a few small resorts, and the village of Lake Ann at the northeastern corner. The lake sits in gentle hills and is wooded all the way around. It's an odd-shaped lake, a crescent with a large rectangular finger to the west and two small extensions at the southern tip. The western one is almost a separate lake. The eastern one provides access via a channel to Mud Lake (one of three Mud Lakes in the county). The Platte River flows through this lake via Mud Lake.

Map of area: goo.gl/maps/ltLtv

DNR map: atic.biz/water_maps/lake_ann.pdf

Lake area: 527 acres   **Shoreline length:** 6.1 miles.

Lake depth: 76 feet in the northwestern half and 71 feet in the southern half. At the center of the "entrance" to the western section, there's a 5-foot-deep shoal; the center of that section reaches 67 feet deep. East of another 5-foot-deep shoal in the center of the main lake the depth reaches 62 feet. There are both shallows and nice drop-offs scattered all around the lake's shore. The eastern extension is 14 feet deep. The western extension, almost its own lake, is 7 feet deep.

Type of bottom: Fibrous peat, gravel, marl, pulpy peat, and sand.

Inlets: At the south end of the lake are two extensions which can be seen here: **goo.gl/maps/03Ctp**

There's a narrow and short channel providing access to the western extension.

At the southeastern corner of the eastern extension is an 800-foot channel providing the only (easy) public access to Mud Lake. Technically, that channel is the Platte River. It first shows up entering in a corner of Mud Lake then flows from that lake to Lake Ann via this channel.
Ransom Creek enters the lake in the center of the east side's southern half.

Outlet: The Platte River exits Lake Ann from the south side of the western finger.

Key features and obstructions: Be aware of the narrow 5-foot shoal in the center of the lake and another shoal the same depth at the center of the "entrance" to the western section.

Like Pearl Lake, there's a complex structure to the shape and bottom of this lake that provides numerous features and obstructions within the lake, too many to easily cover.

Motors allowed: Yes, but there are several "slow, no wake" zones around the shore where the water is 3 feet deep or less. See the map at the launch site for exact locations.

More details for the lake: A popular and fun lake!

Fish typically caught: Bluegill, brown trout, crappie, largemouth bass, northern pike, perch, pumpkinseed, rainbow trout, rock bass, and smallmouth bass. In fact, over 20 different species have been reported.

Where fish are typically found: Look for pike along the drop-off near the western shoreline, in the corner near the boat launch, and in the northwest corner at depths of 20 feet. Look for bass at 10 to 20 feet all around the lake. Panfish seem to like the shallows of much of the southern end, including the two extensions. The big hang-out is at the sunken island, now a 5-foot-deep shoal in the center of the main lake. Most of the species can be found there near the drop-offs all around the shoal and especially to the east and west.

More details for fishing: There are reeds, underwater logs, and water lilies in some of the shallower areas, and areas of moderate vegetation all around the lake. Around the shore it's a scattered mix of shallow/gradual depth areas and quick drop-offs.

Access point: Reynolds Road

- **Details:** DNR access site, hard-surface boat ramp, limited parking, restroom (follow the upper trail along the shore south 400 feet to first campsite encountered at the state park campground).
- **Map:** 44.715519, -85.862254; goo.gl/maps/drW87
- **Directions from Lake Ann:** From the intersection of Maple Street (County Road 610) and 1st Street, take Maple Street 1.1 miles west to (southbound) Reynolds Road. Turn left (south) and go 0.7 miles to the access road for the site. Turn left (east) and go 0.1 miles to the access site.

> FISH TIP: **Northern pike** (a.k.a. great northern pike) are toothy predators commonly associated with weedy shallows of both the Great Lakes and inland waters. In rivers they are often found around log jams or fallen timber. Pike spawn in early spring and are usually found in shallow water. As summer progresses they are found in deeper water, often on the outside edges of deep weed beds. *(Source: Michigan DNR)*

14. Lime Lake

General location: Northeastern area, northwest of Lake Ann village.

General description: Beautiful, quiet, and fairly secluded little lake with no development and wild all around. Nestled in hills, the lake is surrounded by woods and a somewhat open area along the northern half. Immediately to the northwest is an "orphaned" neighbor lake that's about half the size of the main lake.

Map of area: goo.gl/maps/WJgkG

DNR map: atic.biz/water_maps/lime_lake.pdf

Lake area: 15 acres

Shoreline length: 0.8 miles for the main lake, 0.5 miles for the "orphan" lake at the northwest.

Lake depth: 25 feet just east of center, quite deep for its size.

Type of bottom: Marl, organic, and sand.

Inlet: None.   **Outlet:** None.

Motors allowed: Yes, but only a very small motor makes sense because of the unimproved sandy launch area.

More details for the lake: The woods come right to the water's edge along the south side. The north shore is grassy/sandy. Expect a camper or two near the parking areas.

If you like to explore there are three other lakes nearby:

1. An "orphan" lake immediately to the northwest. It's a little lower, much shallower, and about half the area of the main lake.
2. A few hundred feet northeast of the center of the main lake is a small pond that's half an acre in size during high water periods and almost not there during low water periods.
3. When entering on Lime Lake Road, 0.1 miles in on the right (north) there's a small lake that's about 1.5 acres.

Fish typically caught: Bluegill, largemouth bass, northern pike, perch, pumpkinseed, and rock bass, as well as reports of walleye (which are stocked here occasionally).

More details for fishing: The east and west ends have some rushes and tall grasses. There are a some areas of lily pads in the summer. The lake is mostly out of the wind due to the hills on the southern half and surrounding woods.

Access point: Lime Lake Road

- **Details:** No official boat launch just a few unimproved sandy paths to the water's edge, two very small parking areas close together, no restroom. Four-wheel-drive is recommended for travel on Rayle and Lime Lake Roads.
- **Map:** 44.754511, -85.930772; goo.gl/maps/iueh3
- **Directions from Lake Ann:** From the intersection of County Road 610 (Maple Street) and 1st Street, take County Road 610 west 3.2 miles to Maple City Highway. (Along the way, at 1.7 miles you'll curve right (north) on Ole White Drive, then at 2.2 miles you'll turn left (west) on Almira Road.) At the intersection with northbound Maple City Highway (County Road 669) go straight just over 0.1 miles to westbound Almira Road. Turn right (northwest) and go 2.0 miles to (northbound) Rayle Road. Turn right (northeast) and go 0.8 miles to the unsigned Lime Lake Road; along the way you'll curve north then northwest. Turn left (west) and go just under 0.3 miles to the parking areas.

FISH TIP: **Rainbow trout/steelhead** are one of Michigan's favorite sport fish and found all over the state, from inland lakes and streams to the Great Lakes.

Those that live only in streams are called **rainbow trout** and are smaller that their migratory brethren. These scrappy sport fish are found in cooler stream water and deeper lakes, and are highly sought by fly fishermen.

Larger specimens of these fish that are hatched (or stocked) in a river, migrate out to the big water to mature, then return to their natal streams to reproduce have come to be called **steelhead**. They are usually pursued during their spawning runs which begin in late October and continue through early May. With fish that have completed spawning but have yet to migrate back to the big lake (called "drop-backs") and a few summer-run fish, there are almost always some steelhead in the streams. Michigan is one of the best steelhead fishing states in the country and virtually all Great Lake tributaries attract some steelhead. (*Main source: Michigan DNR*)

15. Little Platte Lake

General location: Northwestern area, northwest of Honor.

General description: The third largest in the county, this lake is surrounded by wooded flat land with cottages around 50% of the shoreline. It's undeveloped, otherwise, especially along the east side — which is a wild, marshy area with thick, scrubby woods.

Map of area: goo.gl/maps/ndHtU

DNR map: atic.biz/water_maps/little_platte_lake.pdf

Lake area: 820 acres   **Shoreline length:** 6.2 miles

Lake depth: 7 feet slightly south of the center, very shallow for its size. Most of the lake is between 2 and 5 feet deep. The depth is controlled by the dam on the Deadstream at Deadstream Road.

Type of bottom: Gravel, marl, organic, and sand.

Inlets: Besides the underwater springs there are three inlet creeks, all of which enter on the east side, one on the northern half and two on the southern half. The latter two are two of three channels of the North Branch Platte River. (The third channel of that river enters the lake's outlet about 500 feet downstream from the outlet's source).

Outlet: The lake's outlet at the southeast corner is technically the North Branch Platte River but is known as the Deadstream and is covered in the CREEKS section.

Motors allowed: Yes.

More details for the lake: It's fairly evenly shallow all around the lake. The wild area at the east is home to many swans and other wildlife. Be aware that swans are very protective of their young and can be quite aggressive so it's wise to give them lots of space.

Fish typically caught: Bluegill, crappie, largemouth bass, northern pike, perch, pumpkinseed, and rock bass.

Where fish are typically found: Look for largemouth bass and panfish in the weed beds.

Access points:

A. Saffron Road   B. The Deadstream

Access point details:

A. Little Platte Lake Access — Saffron Road

- **Details:** DNR access site, hard-surface ramp, dock, parking, restroom.
- **Map:** 44.71207, -86.06475; goo.gl/maps/h1J8B
- **Directions from Honor:** From the intersection of Main Street (US-31) and Henry Street, take Main Street 0.1 miles northwest to Deadstream Road (County Road 708). Bear to the right and go 0.9 miles to Indian Hill Road. Turn right (north) and go 3.0 miles to Saffron Road. Turn left (west) and go 1.3 miles to the access road for the site. Turn left (south) and go just over 0.1 miles to the access site.

B. Little Platte Lake Access — The Deadstream

- **Details:** Access by boat by going up the Deadstream.
- **Map:** 44.691144, -86.05774; goo.gl/maps/g4zFM
- **Directions to access:** See access to Deadstream in the CREEKS section.

16. Long Lake

General location: Western central area, northeast of Frankfort and just north of Crystal Lake.

General description: Pretty and unassuming lake, shaped like a leaf or an arrowhead. It's wooded all the way around with hills along much of the south side. Cottages are scattered around half the shoreline; it's wild on the rest.

Map of area: goo.gl/maps/NIEby

Lake area: 328 acres   **Shoreline length:** 3.9 miles

Lake depth: 18 feet in the center of the eastern half, fairly deep for its size. Otherwise, the lake is relatively shallow with sand bars at the northeast and off of two points on the north side.

Type of bottom: Sand, organic.   **Inlets and outlets:** None.

Key obstructions: The sand bars mentioned above and the shallow southeast corner.

Motors allowed: Yes.

Fish typically caught: Bluegill, largemouth bass, northern pike, perch, redear sunfish, and rock bass.

More details for fishing: There are lily pads in the southeast corner and along the shore.

Access point: Long Lake Road

- **Details:** Sand/gravel launch, very limited parking, no restroom.
- **Map:** 44.695586, -86.178106; goo.gl/maps/szpCs
- **Directions from Frankfort:** From the intersection of M-22 (7th Street) and Forest Avenue, take M-22 north 7.9 miles to Long Lake Road. (Along the way you'll travel north, east along Crystal Lake, then north again.) Turn right (east) and go 0.4 miles to the access site.

17. Loon Lake

General location: Northwestern area, northwest of Honor and Platte Lake.

General description: A fun, smaller lake and surprisingly deep. Except for one or two cottages at the southeast it's wild all around. There are mostly woods surrounding the lake with some marsh/wetland on the northeast side. This lake is known as Round Lake on some older maps, which is curious given its somewhat crescent shape. The Lower Platte River flows through this lake and it's in the Sleeping Bear Dunes National Lakeshore.

Note: The use of any area in the Sleeping Bear Dunes National Lakeshore requires a national park pass.

Map of area: goo.gl/maps/gnpp2

DNR map: atic.biz/water_maps/loon_lake.pdf

Lake area: 95 acres   **Shoreline length:** 1.8 miles

Lake depth: 66 feet in southern third, fairly deep for its size. Down the center from north to south, it starts shallow then gradually gets deeper.

Type of bottom: Marl, muck, and sand.

Inlets: There's a minor creek coming in at the center of the west side's southern half. There's a more substantial creek entering a little north of the southwest corner. The Lower Platte River comes in (along with a lot of sand and silt) in the middle of the east side.

Outlet: The Lower Platte River exits the lake at the northwest corner.

Key obstructions: Where the Lower Platte River enters, there's a plume of sand out into the lake making it very shallow there. It's fairly shallow along the northeastern shore as well.

Motors allowed: Yes, but it's a "no wake" lake — any boat with a motor must not exceed a "slow--no wake" speed and there's a speed limit of 5 mph. Note that the Lower Platte River is a "no wake" river, as well.

More details for the lake: The Lower Platte River gets a lot of visitors during the summer, so expect boaters paddling the river to be passing though the northeastern section of the lake.

Fish typically caught: Bluegill, crappie, largemouth bass, northern pike, perch, rainbow trout, rock bass, and smallmouth bass. Other species come through the lake at times via the Lower Plate River, such as salmon and steelhead during their annual spawning runs.

Where fish are typically found: The best fishing is likely on the south and west sides. Look for northerns and panfish near the edges of weed beds. And be sure to check near the river's entrance/exit for what's coming through.

More details for fishing: There are some lily pads near where the creeks enter at the southwest corner. You'll find some sharp drop-offs and fish habitat not too far from the western, southern, and eastern shores.

Access points:

A. Michigan Highway M-22   B. Lower Platte River

Access point details:

A. Loon Lake Access — Michigan Highway M-22

- **Details:** Hard-surface boat ramp with dock, parking for vehicles with trailers, pavilion, picnic tables, restrooms.
- **Map:** 44.708922, -86.126368; goo.gl/maps/TVv9C
- **Directions from Honor:** From the intersection of Main Street (US-31) and Henry Street, take Main Street 0.1 miles northwest to Deadstream Road (County Road 708). Bear to the right and go 5.3 miles to M-22. Turn left (west) and go 1.0 miles to the entrance to the access site on the right (northwest) side of the road.

B. Loon Lake Access — Lower Platte River

- **Details:** Access by boat via the Lower Platte River.
- **Map:** 44.71031, -86.127445; goo.gl/maps/GFCSu
- **Directions to access:** See "Lower Platte River Access — M22 Launch" in the RIVERS section.

18. Lower Herring Lake

General location: Southwestern area, south of Elberta.

General description: Pretty, medium-sized lake with a nice depth. There's some development around the lake — a small resort on the southwest side and south end, some cottages on the south, east and north sides, and a small summer camp at the middle of the west side. Woods surround the lake and go close to the water's edge. There are small hills and dunes on the partially-wild west side.

Map of area: goo.gl/maps/RvmkU

DNR map: atic.biz/water_maps/lower_herring_lake.pdf

Lake area: 450 acres   **Shoreline length:** 3.8 miles

Lake depth: 60 feet in the center of a tall, narrow basin southeast of lake's center. There's a similarly shaped but smaller 56-foot-deep basin northeast of center. There are two small holes deeper than 50 feet just west of center in the northern and southern halves. The dam on the outlet maintains the lake's level.

Type of bottom: Sand, gravel, clay, organic. Look for good gravel and rubble south of the inlet.

Inlet: The 10-foot-wide Herring Creek, coming in from Upper Herring Lake, enters near the center of the northern half of the east side, just south of the Elberta Resort Road access.

Outlet: There's a 0.3-mile outlet to Lake Michigan near the center of the southern half of the west side. There's a small dam 0.1 miles down the outlet.

Motors allowed: Yes.

Fish typically caught: Bluegill, largemouth bass, perch, rock bass, smallmouth bass, walleye, and white sucker. Besides the occasional northern pike, there are salmon and steelhead during their runs.

Where fish are typically found: Look for walleyes in the 50-foot-deep holes off of center in the northern and southern halves, or in about 15 feet of water near the center of the eastern "bay" off of White Owl Road. Find bass along the shoreline. A variety of fish may be found at the drop-offs in the southern half along the west side.

More details for fishing: There are lily pads in the southwest "bay" area and some scattered rushes around the shoreline, but otherwise it's pretty clear. The depths from shore drop off fairly fast all around the lake, especially along the west and south sides, and are almost like ledges in some places.

Access points:

A. Elberta Resort Road
B. White Owl Road
C. Boo Hoo View Road

Access point details:

A. Lower Herring Lake Access — Elberta Resort Road

- **Details:** DNR access site, hard-surface launch, dock, parking for up to 6 vehicles with trailers, no restroom. The Herring Creek inlet is just to the south.
- **Map:** 44.57084, -86.208959; goo.gl/maps/MLyat
- **Directions from Frankfort:** From the intersection of M-115 (Forest Avenue) and M-22 (Lake Street), take M-22 5.2 miles south to Elberta Resort Road. Turn right (west) and go 0.3 miles to the parking lot for the launch site.

B. Lower Herring Lake Access — White Owl Road

- **Details:** Road-end access site, sand/gravel launch, roadside parking, no restroom. The parking lot, pavilion, and picnic tables on the south side of the road are for the White Owl Community Building when it's being used.
- **Map:** 44.564981, -86.205164; goo.gl/maps/tcN1m
- **Directions from Frankfort:** From the intersection of M-115 (Forest Avenue) and M-22 (Lake Street), take M-22 5.6 miles south to White Owl Road. Turn right (west) and go 0.2 miles to the access site.

C. Lower Herring Lake Access — Boo Hoo View Road

- **Details:** Road-end access site, gravel launch. limited parking, no restroom. (A little history — one summer's day in the early 1900s, the young daughter of a Watervale area property owner went exploring the sand dunes on the west side of the lake. The sand was so hot it burned her feet and when came home all she saw was "boo hoo!" At the end of the road is a view of those sand dunes, and the road was named Boo Hoo View.)
- **Map:** 44.557828, -86.210145; goo.gl/maps/HWfVY
- **Directions from Frankfort:** From the intersection of M-115 (Forest Avenue) and M-22 (Lake Street), take M-22 6.1 miles south to Watervale Road. Turn right (west) and go 0.6 miles to Boo Hoo View Road. Go straight (west) less than 0.2 miles to the parking lot for the access site.

19. Mary's Lake

General location: Northeastern area, southwest of Lake Ann village and just west of Lake Ann.

General description: Pretty little gem of a lake. It's surrounded by woods with low hills on the north and south and swampy areas to the east and northwest. There's no development, it's all state land, and the Lake Ann Pathway hiking trail passes close along the south side.

Map of area: goo.gl/maps/TFpWC

Lake area: 7 acres   **Shoreline length:** 0.4 miles

Lake depth: 25 feet, quite deep for its size.

Type of bottom: Organic and muck.

Inlets: At the point on the north side is an inlet creek coming from Tarnwood Lake and other unnamed lakes. In the middle of the east "bay" is an inlet coming from Shavenaugh Lake.

Outlet: At the north in the east "bay" is an outlet that flows straight east to Lake Ann.

Motors allowed: Yes. But only the smallest of motors would be practical on such a small lake and to have to carry down the access path.

Fish typically caught: Bluegill, largemouth bass, and assorted panfish.

More details for fishing: There's lots of shoreline lily pads and downed tree cover.

Access point: Reynolds Road

- **Details:** Simple dirt/mud launch, carry-in access only, limited parking, no restroom. Local folks have put down a few old pallets and wooden dock pieces to improve the launch.
- **Map:** 44.71658, -85.866882; goo.gl/maps/u853T
- **Directions from Lake Ann:** From the intersection of Maple Street (County Road 610) and 1st Street, take Maple Street 1.1 miles west to (southbound) Reynolds Road. Turn left (south) and go 0.6 miles to the unsigned, dirt/gravel Shavenaugh Road on the right (west). Turn right and go about 300 feet to the turn-around. Access to the lake is down the 250-foot dirt path to the southwest.

20. Mud Lake (off of Lake Ann)

General location: Northeastern area, south of Lake Ann village.

General description: A somewhat isolated, smaller lake with gentle hills on two sides and surrounded by woods. It's wild all around except for one or two cottages. A skinny lake with a larger "bubble" section at the southern end, it's one of three Mud Lakes in the county.

Map of area: goo.gl/maps/ZXQ5p

Lake area: 30 acres   **Shoreline length:** 1.4 miles

Lake depth: 5+ feet, on the shallow side for its size. Its deepest points are in the middle when first entering the lake and in the "bubble" section at the southern end.

Type of bottom: Organic and muck.

Inlets: A few small creeks enter the lake at the northeast corner. In the middle of the southeast side of the southern section is a wide inlet creek. Not far away, just 300 feet to the southwest and a few hundred feet from the southern tip, the Platte River enters the lake.

Outlet: The Platte River exits the lake via the outlet channel at the middle of the west side. (The river then travels through Lake Ann.)

Motors allowed: Yes.

More details for the lake: A railroad once passed along this lake on its way to Lake Ann. The path where it ran is still there on the southwest side. The stubs of the pilings for the crossing are still present in the west end of the channel going out to Lake Ann.

Fish typically caught: Bluegill, crappie, largemouth bass, perch, and possibly many of the same species that Lake Ann offers.

More details for fishing: There are some lily pads in the shallow areas of the southern section.

More details for paddling: You can try to paddle up the two inlets that enter the "bubble" section at the south, but you won't get too far due to shallow water and lots of mud and muck.

Access point: Outlet channel from Lake Ann
- **Details:** The only (easy) public access to the lake is to go up the 800-foot channel (technically the Platte River) from the eastern extension of Lake Ann.

- **Map:** 44.704198, -85.840633; goo.gl/maps/vtIY1
- **Directions to access:** See access for Lake Ann.

21. Mud Lake (near the Lower Platte River)

General location: Northwestern area, northwest of Honor and Platte Lake.

General description: Here's an interesting lake. It's another of three Mud Lakes in the county and this one lives up to its name. There's a reason it looks so dark in satellite photos, and it's not due to depth. A pretty locale, the lake is wild all the way around and surrounded by woods and some small marsh areas. And it's in the Sleeping Bear Dunes National Lakeshore.

Note: The use of any area in the Sleeping Bear Dunes National Lakeshore requires a national park pass.

Map of area: goo.gl/maps/VKOrT

Lake area: 59 acres   **Shoreline length:** 1.2 miles

Lake depth: Less than 2 feet, extremely shallow for a lake its size. The depth at this lake is found around the edges where it reaches close to 2 feet in some areas. But beyond about 15 feet from shore and throughout the main area of the lake it's only a few inches deep (at least near the end of a dry 2012 summer). As for the bottom — the mud and muck below the water — its depth is hard to determine.

Type of bottom: Mostly muck, some sand.

Inlets: None.

Outlet: In the southeast corner there's an 600-foot outlet providing access to and from the Lower Platte River. Watch for very shallow water near the shore on either side of the entrance to the outlet.

Key features: The surprising and consistent shallowness of this lake with such a large area and the seemingly bottomless mucky bottom throughout most of the lake make it unique.

Key obstructions: Its key feature is also its biggest obstruction; most of the central area of the lake is very shallow and very mucky.

Motors allowed: No.

More details for the lake: There is plenty of educational value to this lake for those studying lakes, and certainly some "entertainment" and aesthetic value. Its usefulness for much else seems quite limited.

Fish typically caught: In fact, there were some medium-sized largemouth bass observed, but in general, this lake appears to have little value for fishing.

More details for fishing: There are woods and shrubs up to the water's edge and some lily pads along the northwest side in summer.

More details for paddling: The best bet is to stay very close to the shore. In the middle of the lake and near some of the shore, there is not much water and a lot of oatmeal-like muck — offering a good work-out. Perhaps in a wet spring this lake would have some navigable depth to it and would be fun to explore.

Access points:

A. Lake Michigan Road
B. Mud Lake Outlet into the Lower Platte River

Access point details:

A. **Mud Lake (near LPR) Access — Lake Michigan Road**
- **Details:** Sand/dirt launch, carry-in access only via a 250-foot path, roadside parking, no restroom.
- **Map:** 44.719671, -86.128424; goo.gl/maps/oRkom
- **Directions from Honor:** From the intersection of Main Street (US-31) and Henry Street, take Main Street 0.1

miles northwest to Deadstream Road (County Road 708). Bear to the right and go 5.3 miles to M-22. Turn left (west) and go 0.6 miles to Lake Michigan Road. Turn right (north) and go 0.8 miles to the access path on the left (west) side of the road.

At Lake Michigan Road you may have to hunt for the path; it's wide and seldom-used gently curving through the woods. It starts 750 feet south of Weir Road and just north of a point directly across from (northern) Park Road — there on the right (east). (Note that there's another path to the lake a few hundred feet to the south but its access at the lake is poor.)

B. Mud Lake (near LPR) Access — Mud Lake Outlet from the Lower Platte River

- **Details:** Paddle up the 600-foot outlet creek from the Lower Platte River. (The creek is actually deeper than the lake in some places.) Expect to maneuver through and around a few fallen trees.
- **Map:** 44.715655, -86.128312; goo.gl/maps/TzvNf
- **Directions to the outlet creek:** See "Lower Platte River Access — M22 Launch" in the RIVERS section. Put in at M-22 — the outlet is downriver just 0.6 miles. Or, put in at the Loon Lake launch and paddle up the Lower Platte River for just 0.4 miles. The current is typically slow enough that this is not hard to do.

FISH TIP: Although **Walleyes** are usually associated with the bottom, the most active are sometimes suspended in the water column. These fish are photosensitive. Fishing for them is often best early and late in shallow water, though that is less critical in deep water. But, walleyes often move shallow to feed at night and casting with artificial lures or drifting with live bait should produce walleyes after dark. *(Source: Michigan DNR)*

22. Mud Lake (off of Sanford Lake)

General location: Northeastern area, southwest of Lake Ann village and Lake Ann.

General description: The third of three Mud Lakes in the county, this is a mostly wild, smaller lake with woods on three sides and gentle hills on the north and east. There are only five cottages on the lake and the east half is surrounded by state land. It's accessed via Sanford Lake.

Map of area: goo.gl/maps/Pdbjq

Lake area: 12 acres   **Shoreline length:** 0.5 miles

Lake depth: 10+ feet (likely much more), fairly deep for its size.

Type of bottom: Some sand around the edges, otherwise organic.

Inlet: None.

Outlet: There's a short outlet at the northwest connecting to Sanford Lake.

Motors allowed: Yes. But like its larger neighbor immediately to the west, it's a "no wake" lake.

More details for the lake: The water has a rich deep red/brown color which appears to be from tannins in decaying wood and vegetation in and around the lake. It's interesting because the deep color dies out at the end of the lake's outlet.

In the spring of 2013 there was a large beaver lodge on south end. Parts of the area are a nice "sanctuary" for wildlife, including birds, beaver, deer, porcupines, and otter.

Fish typically caught: Bluegill, largemouth bass, green sunfish, northern pike, perch, rock bass, and smallmouth bass.

More details for fishing: There's some scattered tree-fall, hedges, and rushes around the shoreline.

Access point: Short outlet channel from Sanford Lake.

- **Details:** The only public access is via a short, narrow, and shallow outlet channel from the east side of Sanford Lake. It appears that during low water levels the channel might not be deep enough to travel through. There's a footbridge over the channel and a park for local residents on either side.
- **Map:** 44.699002, -85.854666; goo.gl/maps/HxsxQ
- **Directions to access:** See access for Sanford Lake.

23. Otter Lake

General location: Near northwestern corner, north of Honor.

General description: Picturesque smaller, clear-water lake in the Sleeping Bear Dunes National Lakeshore surrounded by woods and small hills. Except for a few remaining cottages, it's wild all around.

Note: The use of any area in the Sleeping Bear Dunes National Lakeshore requires a national park pass.

Map of area: goo.gl/maps/XehTY

Lake area: 64 acres   **Shoreline length:** 1.4 miles

Lake depth: 15+ feet (likely much more). Fairly deep for its size.

Type of bottom: Sand, organic, muck.

Inlet: There's an inlet in the middle of the south side coming in from Bass Lake.

Outlet: There's an outlet west of the middle of the north side. North of the lake about 1000 feet it joins with springs and smaller creeks to become Otter Creek (covered in the CREEKS section).

Key obstructions: There are some fallen trees around the shoreline.

Motors allowed: No.

More details for the lake: This lake is part of a succession of connected lakes and creeks that starts with Deer Lake and Bass Lake to the south, an 1100-foot creek from Bass to Otter Lake, then out via Otter Creek at the north to Lake Michigan.

Fish typically caught: Bluegill, largemouth bass, northern pike, perch, rock bass, and smallmouth bass.

More details for fishing: Like its southern neighbor Bass Lake, around most of the edges the depth drops off quickly to 6 to 10 feet. There's lots of fish habitat scattered around the edges such as fallen trees, rushes, and a few areas of lily pads.

Access point: Trails End Road.

- **Details:** Sand/dirt launch, small dock. parking for two vehicles, no restroom.
- **Map:** 44.737816, -86.061193; goo.gl/maps/8nl5y
- **Directions from Honor:** From the intersection of Main Street (US-31) and Henry Street, take Main Street 0.1 miles northwest to Deadstream Road (County Road 708). Bear to the right and go 0.9 miles to Indian Hill Road. Turn right (north) and go 4.5 miles to Trails End Road. Turn left (west) and go 0.5 miles to an "S" turn in M-22. Go straight (west) on M-22 just over 0.1 miles to the west part of Trails End Road. Keep going straight (west) and follow the road 0.7 miles through a right then a left turn to the access road for the launch on the right (north) side of the road. Turn right (north) and go 300 feet to the access site.

24. Pearl Lake

General location: Northeastern area, northwest of Lake Ann village.

General description: A very irregularly-shaped, medium-sized, spring-fed lake. It looks like many interconnected pieces and has a lot of shoreline for its area. There are some cottages on the northern portions of the lake; it's wild on the other parts. The Pearl Lake Natural Area is at the southern end. The lake is very much subject to seasonal and year-to-year climate conditions.

Map of area: goo.gl/maps/mzUYU

Lake area: 350 acres. (This is an estimate based on nearby lakes similar in size, April, 2012.)

Shoreline length: 7.6 miles, but does not include the islands, and measured during the lake's "lower" level (April, 2012). During higher levels there are several places where the lake's area and shoreline is noticeably larger. (Although fingers and islands would be smaller, of course.)

Lake depth: 15 feet average, deeper in a few holes (like the east end and main portion in the northwestern corner), but many areas of the lake will be shallower. Current climate conditions have a significant effect on the water level.

Type of bottom: Organic, muck, and sand around some of the shoreline.

Inlets and outlets: None.

Key features and obstructions: Like Lake Ann, but even more so, there's such a complexity to the shape and bottom structure that it provides many features and obstructions within the lake, too numerous to easily cover.

Motors allowed: Yes, but some areas are "no wake" zones and some are too shallow or filled with plant life.

More details for the lake: The lake is home to loons, bald eagles, and osprey. There's a protected loon nest in the southern portion of the lake and it's a "no wake" zone. There's an osprey nest in the eastern finger of the lake.

Fish typically caught: Bluegill, crappie, largemouth bass, northern pike, perch, and rock bass.

More details for fishing: With a little exploration you'll find many features, bottom types, and forms of fish habitat.

More details for paddling: This lake is such an odd shape with so many interconnecting pieces it's fun to explore. But, traveling in a few areas may be difficult during low water periods due to shallow conditions and a lot of aquatic plant life.

Access points:

A. Wagner Road   B. Rayle Road

Access point details:

A. Pearl Lake Access — Wagner Road

- **Details:** Gravel launch, limited parking, no restroom. Use this site for trailerable boats.
- **Map:** 44.76835, -85.918307; goo.gl/maps/dCqI3
- **Directions from Lake Ann:** From the intersection of County Road 610 (Maple Street) and 1st Street, take County Road 610 west 3.2 miles to Maple City Highway. (Along the way, at 1.7 miles you'll curve right (north) on Ole White Drive, then at 2.2 miles you'll turn left (west) on Almira Road.) At Maple City Highway (County Road 669) turn right (north) and go 2.2 miles to Wagner Road. Turn left (west) and go 1.2 miles to the entrance to the access site on the left (south) side of the road. The boat launch is about 400 feet to the south. (There is also access to Wagner Road just 0.1 miles from the south end of Pearl Lake Road. From there take Wagner Road 0.1 miles east to the access site entrance.)

B. Pearl Lake Access — Rayle Road

- **Details:** Sand/dirt launch, carry-in access only, very limited parking, no restroom. This launch may be difficult to use during the lake's low water periods. Expect lots of aquatic plant life here before getting to the open water. Four-wheel-drive is recommended for travel on Rayle Road.
- **Map:** 44.756383, -85.925869; goo.gl/maps/vCyAh
- **Directions from Lake Ann:** From the intersection of County Road 610 (Maple Street) and 1st Street, take County Road 610 west 3.2 miles to Maple City Highway. (Along the way, at 1.7 miles you'll curve right (north) on Ole White Drive, then at 2.2 miles you'll turn left (west) on Almira Road.) At the intersection with northbound Maple City Highway (County Road 669) go straight just over 0.1 miles to westbound Almira Road. Turn right (northwest) and go 2.0 miles to (northbound) Rayle Road. Turn right (northeast) and go 1.0 mile to the access site on the right (east). (Along the way the road curves north then northwest. The access site is 0.2 miles past the unsigned and westbound Lime Lake Road.)

25. Platte Lake

General location: Northwestern area, northwest of Honor.

General description: The second largest lake in the county, it's also known as Big Platte Lake — to differentiate it from its northern neighbor, Little Platte Lake. There are cottages and small lakeside resorts around most of the lake and flat wooded property around all of the lake. Beautiful clear water and lovely area, this is likely the second most sought-after location in the area after Crystal Lake.

Map of area: goo.gl/maps/TQRvC

DNR map: atic.biz/water_maps/platte_lake.pdf

Lake area: 2516 acres   **Shoreline length:** 9.1 miles

Lake depth: There's a 90-foot hole near the northwest end and a 70-foot hole just west of the center. All along the northeast side there's a wide shoulder; the change in depth from the shore is initially fairly gradual before a mild drop-off. On the other hand, along the south side and especially on the west portions of the lake the depth changes rapidly from the shore to the deepest points.

Type of bottom: Gravel, sand, marl, and muck.

Inlet: The Upper Platte River enters at the east end.

Outlet: The outlet at the northwest corner is the start of the Lower Platte River.

Motors allowed: Yes.

More details for the lake: The Platte River flows through this lake providing it with a relatively quick turnover of fresh water. Several times more often, in fact, than that of its much larger, clear-water, southern neighbor Crystal Lake.

And, like Crystal Lake, expect plenty of activity on this lake in the summer, such as motor boats, water skiers, jet skis, pontoon boats, sailboats, kayaks, paddle boards, and swimmers. But, rarely are there many boats at one time. Look for fishing boats in spring, summer, and fall, and ice fishermen in mid to late winter.

Fish typically caught: Bluegill, crappie, northern pike, perch, (bigger) smallmouth bass, and walleye are common. Expect channel catfish, largemouth bass, pumpkinseed, and rock bass as well. There's also the occasional chinook and coho salmon, steelhead/rainbow trout, and (some big) brown trout.

Where fish are typically found: Look for walleyes in the deeper areas of the northwestern end. Seek out bass and panfish along the western side. Find smallmouth bass on the north side of the east end, rocky spots along the north shore, and drop-offs anywhere in the lake. Look for northerns near the edges of weed beds in the southeastern area near where the river enters the lake, as well as in 12 to 15 feet of water around Birch Point and the DNR access site at Arborvitae Drive. The inlet and outlet of the Platte River are generally good places to start.

More details for paddling: This is a larger lake with many paddling uses, such as a quiet sunset paddle on a calm evening or sea kayaking all around the lake.

Access points:

A. Arborvitae Drive
B. Lake Street
C. Deadstream Road
D. Upper Platte River

Access point details:

A. Platte Lake Access — Arborvitae Drive

- **Details:** DNR boat launch, hard-surface ramp for up to medium-sized boats on a trailer, short dock, parking, restroom. Some folks doing a Lower Platte River trip start here to get in ALL of the river.
- **Map:** 44.696167, -86.120718; goo.gl/maps/kEhVy
- **Directions from Honor:** From the intersection of US-31 (Main Street) and Henry Street, take US-31 1.3 miles west to Platte Road. Turn right (west) and go 4.4 miles to Arborvitae Road. Turn right (north) and go 0.2 miles to the access site on the right (east) side of the road.

B. Platte Lake Access — Lake Street

- **Details:** Very simple road-end access, carry-in access only, no parking, no restroom. The road ends at a three-foot beach and that's it, no boat launch. The site is only as wide as the road and there's no parking at the site or immediately nearby.
- **Map:** 44.675255, -86.078730; goo.gl/maps/HiXfg
- **Directions from Honor:** From the intersection of US-31 (Main Street) and Henry Street, take US-31 1.3 miles west to Platte Road. Turn right (west) and go 1.7 miles to Lake Street. Turn right (north) and go less than 0.2 miles to the access site at the road's end.

C. Platte Lake Access — **Deadstream** Road
- **Details:** Sand/dirt launch, carry-in access only, very limited parking, no restroom. Small, empty piece of property between the road and the lake.
- **Map:** 44.684906, -86.062177; goo.gl/maps/QJVXs
- **Directions from Honor:** From the intersection of Main Street (US-31) and Henry Street, take Main Street 0.1 miles northwest to Deadstream Road (County Road 708). Bear to the right and go 2.3 miles and watch for where the Deadstream passes under the road. Go another 750 feet to the access site on left (southwest) side of the road.

D. Platte Lake Access — Upper Platte River
- **Details:** Access by boat coming in via the Upper Platte River. (There's probably little advantage to using the river to access the lake over the easier and more direct Deadstream Road access mentioned just above.)
- **Map:** 44.68152, -86.06554; goo.gl/maps/KPGr5
- **Directions to access:** See "Upper Platte River Access — Deadstream Road" in the RIVERS section.

26. Round Lake

General location: Western central area, northeast of Frankfort and just north of Crystal Lake.

General description: Scenic little lake in the Sleeping Bear Dunes National Lakeshore. It's wild all around, surrounded by woods on the northern half and marsh and wetland on the southern half.

Note: The use of any area in the Sleeping Bear Dunes National Lakeshore requires a national park pass.

Map of area: goo.gl/maps/jmxwd

Lake area: 15 acres   **Shoreline length:** 0.7 miles

Lake depth: 6+ feet. The main depth is in a central hole. The change in depth from shore is fairly quick on the north side but more gradual on the west, south, and east sides.

Type of bottom: Sand, muck, and organic. The bottom along the north side is very hard. But, beware of the deceptively false bottom along the east, south, and west sides of the lake; the mixture of material there can be over 6 feet deep.

Inlet: There's a tiny inlet creek at the southwest corner.

Outlet: Just west of the southeast corner is Round Lake Creek that flows into Crystal Lake to the south.

Motors allowed: No.

More details for the lake: There's some aquatic growth on the west, south, and east sides. The marshland to the south shows this lake was more than three times its current size in years past. In fact, this lake is a former bay of Crystal Lake (before Crystal was lowered about 20 feet in 1873) and still feeds its much larger southern neighbor via the tiny Round Lake Creek outlet. (This is the only lake that feeds Crystal Lake.)

Fish typically caught: Bluegill, green sunfish, largemouth bass, perch, pumpkinseed, and rock bass.

More details for paddling: During low-water periods the shallow water and muck on the south side of the lake will keep you from going into the inlet or outlet creek areas.

Access point: Michigan Highway M-22

- **Details:** Narrow sand/dirt launch, carry-in access only, no restroom, and no parking — just two turn-around slots. It's very shallow and there's lots of gravel in the lake at the launch area.
- **Map:** 44.694196, -86.186638; goo.gl/maps/47B6Q
- **Directions from Frankfort:** From the intersection of M-22 (7th Street) and Forest Avenue, go north on M-22

Street 7.8 miles to the lake's access road on the right (east) side of the street. (Along the way you'll go north, east along Crystal Lake, then north again. You'll see Round Lake on the right just before coming to the access road for the site. If you get to Long Lake Road you've gone 0.1 miles too far.) 130 feet down the access road is the boat launch.

> **FISH TIP: Yellow perch** are one of the most frequently caught fish in Michigan and certainly among the top choices as table fare. They are widespread denizens of both the Great Lakes and inland waters. Perch travel in schools, sometimes very large numbers, and can often be caught all day long without ever moving the boat. Although commonly associated with deep water, perch can actually be found at almost any depth, from just above rubble or rocky bottoms in deep water to around weed beds in shallower lakes. *(Main source: Michigan DNR)*

27. Sanford Lake

General location: Northeastern area and southwest of Lake Ann village and Lake Ann.

General description: A lovely, clear-water, "sock-shaped" lake surrounded by woods and gentle hills. Perhaps 40% is lightly developed with homes and cottages set back from the shore on the hillside. There's access to Mud Lake (one of three in the county) via the channel to the east.

Map of area: goo.gl/maps/tDJjG

Lake area: 50 acres   **Shoreline length:** 1.6 miles

Lake depth: 20+ feet, deep for it's size. There are nice drop-offs from shore, most are in the northern half, There are some more-gradual drop-offs in the southern half.

Type of bottom: Some sand around the edges, otherwise mostly organic.

Inlet: On the east side is an inlet coming in from Mud Lake.

Outlet: None.

Motors allowed: Yes, but it's a "no wake" lake.

Fish typically caught: Bluegill, largemouth bass, green sunfish, northern pike, perch, rock bass, and smallmouth bass.

More details for fishing: There's some scattered tree-fall, hedges, and rushes around the shoreline.

Access point: Reynolds Road

- **Details:** Dirt/mud launch, limited parking, no restroom. It's recommended to back in the final piece of the access road if you have a trailer. Also, do not block access for others — park in the open area out by Reynolds Road.
- **Map:** 44.696661, -85.862006; goo.gl/maps/t4nQ6
- **Directions from Lake Ann:** From the intersection of Maple Street (County Road 610) and 1st Street, take Maple Street 1.1 miles west to (southbound) Reynolds Road. Turn left (south) and go 2.1 miles to the gravel access road on the left (northeast). Turn left and go 450 feet down the access road to the access point.

28. Stevens Lake

General location: Northeastern area, northwest of Lake Ann village.

General description: A very pretty, clear-water, smaller, rectangular-shaped lake, nestled in rolling hills and woods and sheltered from the wind. There are about a dozen cottages on the east and west sides of the lake and a small, private RV park on the northwest corner. All around the lake woods come down to the shore and there are lots of hedges at the edges.

Map of area: goo.gl/maps/kML0b

DNR map: atic.biz/water_maps/stevens_lake.pdf

Lake area: 45 acres   **Shoreline length:** 1.2 miles

Lake depth: 57 feet near the center of the southern half, quite deep for its size. The change in depth is gradual on the north and northwest sides but drops off fast from shore around the other sides of the lake.

Type of bottom: Organic and sand. Hard sand bottom near the shore for much of the lake, but then it's organic on north side, away from shore, and throughout the center.

Inlets and outlets: None.

Key feature: There's a 200-foot finger of land north of center on the west side.

Motors allowed: Yes, but it's a "no wake" lake.

Fish typically caught: Bluegill, crappie, largemouth bass, perch, and rock bass.

More details for fishing: Besides a few scattered patches of lily pads and rushes/cattails there's not a lot plant life along the shore. But there is a fair amount of fallen trees and branches in the water near the shore offering some nice habitat.

Access point: Stevens Lake Road

- **Details:** DNR access site, hard-surface launch, limited parking, restroom.
- **Map:** 44.7589, -85.872214; goo.gl/maps/sX4t8
- **Directions from Lake Ann:** From the intersection of County Road 610 (Maple Street) and 1st Street, take County Road 610 west 1.7 miles to Ole White Drive. Curve right (north) and go 2.1 miles to Stevens Lake Road. Turn right (northeast) and go 0.3 miles to the access road for the site. Turn right (west) and go 0.1 miles to the boat launch.

29. Turtle Lake

General location: Southeastern area, west of Bendon.

General description: A smaller, popular, spring-fed, "up north" lake. There's a fair number of cottages and a small campground on the lake but is otherwise surrounded by woods.

Map of area: goo.gl/maps/dh82z

DNR map: atic.biz/water_maps/turtle_lake.pdf

Lake area: 38 acres   **Shoreline length:** 1.4 miles

Lake depth: Fairly deep for its size — 22 feet near the center of the southeastern half, 19 feet near the center of the northwestern half. There's a shallow (less than 5 feet) bar across the lake between the two halves.

Type of bottom: Marl, organic, and sand.

Inlets and outlets: None.

Key features: In the northwestern half of the lake there's a significantly wide shoulder out to 5 feet deep.

Motors allowed: Yes

Fish typically caught: Bluegill, crappie, largemouth bass, northern pike, perch, rock bass, and walleye.

Where fish are typically found: Look for walleyes in the southeastern hole and bass at the edges of weed beds. Bluegills are in and around the weeds.

Access point: Miller Road

- **Details:** DNR access site, sand/gravel launch, limited vehicle and trailer parking, restroom.
- **Map:** 44.619683, -85.908851; goo.gl/maps/i6Swv
- **Directions from Honor:** From the intersection of US-31 (Main Street) and Henry Street, take US-31 4.1 miles east to Thompsonville Road (southbound County Road

669). Turn right (south) and go 2.6 miles south to Cinder Road. Turn left (east) and go 1.4 miles to Miller Road. Turn right (south) and go 0.2 miles to the access road for the site. Turn left (southeast) and go 250 feet to the launch.

30, 31. Twin and Upper Twin Lakes

General location: Near the southeastern corner, northeast of Nessen City.

General description: The only public access to these lakes is by paddling up Pickerel Creek from the Betsie River. So for those willing to paddle "a little ways," you'll be rewarded with these two little beauties. Surrounded by wetland and further back by woods, there's no development at all on these lakes (other than what the beavers build on Pickerel Creek). Twin Lake is encountered first, then Upper Twin lies directly to the east. The two are connected via a 950-foot channel. It's a wonderful wild area.

Map of area: goo.gl/maps/F1xtk

Lake area: Twin: 16 acres, Upper Twin: 16 acres.

Shoreline length: Twin: 3715 feet, Upper Twin: 3755 ft.

Lake depth: Twin: 15+ feet, Upper Twin: 8+ feet.

Type of bottom: Organic, sand, and muck.

Upper Twin Lake — Inlets: There's a creek-fed 0.25-mile-long channel leading to private residences coming in from the east. There are a few small streams coming in near the middle of the north and south sides.

Upper Twin Lake — Outlet: At the west end there's a 950-foot channel leading to Twin Lake.

Twin Lake — Inlets: At the east end there's the 950-foot channel coming in from Upper Twin Lake. At the point in the shore on the southwest a fairly large stream comes in

(Upper Pickerel Creek, actually). Other smaller streams enter at the south and west.

Twin Lake — Outlet: The outlet (Pickerel Creek) exits at the northeast corner.

Key feature/concern: With the building of the Grass Lake Dam, the water in the Betsie River above the dam, Grass Lake, Grass Lake Creek, Pickerel Creek, and the Twin Lakes was raised a few feet. This makes for easy traveling but there's no solid ground along the shore on any of these bodies of water. What might appear to be land is really a floating mat of loosely interwoven vegetation. So plan accordingly for lunch break, rest stops, etc.

Motors allowed: Yes, but using a motorized boat on Pickerel Creek is not at all practical. (The creek is best done in a kayak.)

More details for the area: It's an interesting place. The source of the Little Betsie River and the division between the Little Betsie River watershed and the main Betsie River watershed is not far away. Upper Pickerel Creek — as mentioned earlier that enters Twin Lake — starts at a point that's very near the dividing line between the two watersheds. A few hundred feet away from that is the source for the Little Betsie River. It joins the main Betsie River several miles to the west. On the other hand, the main Pickerel Creek — the outlet for the Twin Lakes — also flows into the main Betsie River but takes a much different path, connecting to the river a few miles to the north.

Fish typically caught: Bluegill, largemouth bass, northern pike, perch, and rock bass.

More details for fishing: **Twin:** There's not much plant life along the shore. **Upper Twin:** There is some plant life near the shore and lots of partially dissolved algae suspended in the water.

Access point: The only public access to these lakes is via Pickerel Creek off of the Betsie River just above Grass Lake Dam. See access for Pickerel Creek in the CREEKS section.

32. Upper Herring Lake

General location: Southwestern area, southeast of Elberta.

General description: This crescent-shaped lake is the fourth largest in the county. There are cottages on the north and east and a few on the south side. Hills are found to the north, east, and south of the lake, and wild wetland and woods to the west. Like most in the county, the lake is surrounded by wooded property.

Map of area: goo.gl/maps/LbbgA

DNR map: atic.biz/water_maps/upper_herring_lake.pdf

Lake area: 565 acres   **Shoreline length:** 4.1 miles

Lake depth: 26 feet in the center, shallow for its size. There are wide, shallow shoulders on the north and east sides, and quicker drop-offs on the south and west sides. 70% of the lake's interior is 20 to 25 feet deep.

Type of bottom: Sand, gravel, marl, organic, and muck. In shallower water, 40% is sand, rubble, and gravel; 60% is muck and marl. In deeper water, the bottom is 50% sand and 50% marl.

Inlets: The upper portion of Herring Creek enters the lake in the middle of the east side. There's a small creek that enters near the southwest corner.

Outlets: Herring Creek exits in the northwest corner; it's covered in the CREEKS section.

Key obstructions: There are some logs and stumps close to the western shore and along the southern shore.

Motors allowed: Yes.

More details for the lake: The Upper Herring Lake Preserve is on the west side of the lake — a nice wild area.

Fish typically caught: Bluegill, crappie, largemouth bass (less likely than smallmouth), northern pike, perch, rock bass, smallmouth bass, and walleye. There are reports of a few occasional salmon and steelhead that during their runs make it from Lake Michigan, over the dam, through Lower Herring Lake, and up Herring Creek to this lake.

Where fish are typically found: Popular fisheries are the Herring Creek inlet at the eastern tip and the reeds and weed beds to the northeast, at the southwestern tip, and around the entrance to the outlet at the northwest corner. At the deepest part at the lake's center is a spring that attracts bass and walleyes in the warmth of summer.

More details for fishing: There are rushes, weed beds, and aquatic growth scattered around the lake's shoreline. Some logs and stumps are found close to the west side and along the southern shore. There are lily pads, rushes, and other aquatic growth near the entrance to the outlet. Submerged weeds are common around the lake.

More details for paddling: You can explore the inlet (yet it's difficult to get very far), the outlet (a.k.a. Herring Creek — see the CREEKS section), or all around the lake — it's pleasant 2-hour paddle on a gentle summer evening.

Access point: Herron Road

- **Details:** DNR access site, hard-surface launch with short dock, parking for a few vehicles with trailers and a few without, restroom. The water at the launch area can be very shallow in which case a motor cannot be used until several yards from shore. There's also a lot of rushes here but with an open channel through them.
- **Map:** 44.570675, -86.185794; goo.gl/maps/re3z2
- **Directions from Frankfort:** From the intersection of M-115 (Forest Avenue) and M-22 (Lake Street), take M-22 4.5 miles south to Herron Road. Turn left (east) and go 1.2 miles to the access road for the launch site. Turn right (south) and go less than 0.1 miles to the launch.

FISH TIP: The **Sunfish family** — **bluegill, green sunfish, pumpkinseed, redear, rock bass,** and **warmouth** — are a favorite fish in Michigan. Small but prolific, they are found virtually everywhere in the state. They are often the first fish an angler catches and are often sought throughout one's career.

Sunfish are usually associated with cover. They travel in schools and can be found in both rivers and lakes. They spawn in the spring and are easily taken during the bedding season. Community nesters, most sunfish make their beds in the shallows.

Bluegill, the most commonly pursued fish, are the most abundant and are usually found throughout the year around aquatic vegetation.

Green sunfish, rock bass, and **warmouth** (also known as goggle-eyes) have larger mouths than other sunfish species. They are usually associated with cover and found more often around brush or rocks than the other species. They are often taken incidentally by bass fishermen.

Pumpkinseeds, also known as the common sunfish or just plain sunfish, are popular panfish that tend to stay in shallower water than their more popular cousin, the bluegill. They prefer weed patches, sunken logs, or docks for cover. "Pumpkins" are community nesters with spawning beginning in late May. They are often taken from the same areas as bluegills when bedding. In lakes with populations of both sunfish, a typical catch will include members of both species.

Redear sunfish are more often associated with woody debris and/or open water than bluegills or pumpkinseeds (which prefer vegetation). Anglers typically fish for redears on the bottom rather than higher in the water column.

Rock bass: commonly called "red-eye bass," are a hearty panfish. Not usually targeted by anglers, they are often caught incidentally by those seeking much larger bass. They are easy to catch and are a fun, scrappy fish on the hook. Rock bass are often found around stone rubble or large rocks, though they can also be caught in weed beds or around submerged brush. Like other sunfish, rock bass move shallow to spawn and are often caught by crappie fishermen in spring. They may be found in association with smallmouth bass. As table fare they are comparable to other sunfish. *(Main source: Michigan DNR)*

A Place for Your Notes....

Made in the USA
San Bernardino, CA
17 August 2014